TOGETHER TOWARD HOPE

Together Toward Hope

A JOURNEY TO MORAL THEOLOGY

Philip J. Rossi, S.J.

UNIVERSITY OF NOTRE DAME PRESS
NOTRE DAME   LONDON

Library of Congress Cataloging in Publication Data

Rossi, Philip J.
    Together toward hope.

    Includes bibliographical references and index.
    1. Christian ethics — Catholic authors. 2. Social
ethics. 3. Liberty. 4. Imagination. 5. Hope.
I. Title.
BJ1249.R82 1983   241'.042   83-1279
ISBN 0-268-01844-8

Manufactured in the United States of America

Contents

Publication of this volume is
assisted by a grant from the
Catholic Theological Society of America

Preface

Four ideas — freedom, community, imagination, and hope — have preoccupied much of my teaching, writing, and way of living during the last half-dozen years. My efforts to understand these ideas have resulted in the conviction that they play — not merely singly, but also in relationship to one another — a central role in forming and sustaining the reality of human moral life. The contents of this book, therefore, present the account I have been able to develop of how freedom, community, imagination, and hope mutually give moral shape to our human world.

Particular contexts of life and work have formed my dealings with these ideas. By taking brief note now of the most important of them I hope to provide some clues to help the reader see the contours of the intellectual terrain on which my account of these ideas is located.

One important context has been provided by the fact that, although my primary academic training has been in the discipline of philosophy, I have been a faculty member of a department of theology since the completion of my doctoral studies. In consequence, my efforts to understand freedom, community, imagination, and hope in their relation to one another have been shaped by a concomitant effort to sort out the relationships among those forms of inquiry that lay claim to the name "philosophy" and those that lay claim to the name "theology."

This context has had its most direct impact upon the shape given to the central argument of this work, found in chapters 2, 3, and 4. I have tried to shape that argument as a working example of one form of congruence between philosophy and theology. In particular, I have tried to shape that argument to show

how a philosophical rendering of human moral reality opens up for us a region of theological possibilities. The particular philosophical rendering of human moral reality that I offer centers on the claim that the fundamental elements of that reality necessitate that we acknowledge our likeness to one another and that we go on together as a community. The interrelationship between two of the ideas that preoccupy me—freedom and community—plays a central role in explicating this claim. It is, nonetheless, their relationships to the third idea—imagination—that then allow the argument to turn to a consideration of theological possibilities. Imagination provides the context for acknowledging the fourth idea—hope—as the appropriate representation of the possibilities of grace that God evokes from the fundamental elements of our human moral reality.

I have described the movement of my argument—from moral reality to hope—in terms which may have already suggested to some readers a second important context that has shaped this work: the set of philosophical and theological issues about the form and significance of human moral life that are raised in the writings of Immanuel Kant. My reading of these issues has not been unaffected, of course, by other influences—most notably by what I have come to understand of the philosophical concerns explored in the works of Martin Heidegger and of Ludwig Wittgenstein, and by my initial training in neo-scholastic philosophy in the tradition of Joseph Maréchal. In consequence, some may find—not without justification—that my use of Kant is perplexing when compared to the interpretations of Kant that have prevailed in the English-speaking world. Some others, particularly within my own tradition of Roman Catholic theology, may find an effort to place the enterprise of moral theology into a Kantian framework—whether or not it is an "orthodox" interpretation of Kant—to be itself a perplexing, if not misguided, enterprise.

I do not anticipate an easy resolution of either perplexity— and certainly not by remarks offered in a preface. I do suspect, however, that an initial step toward resolution can be taken by noting one Kantian theme that I have found to be common to the thinkers whom I have perceived as helping me give shape to this work: a concern to recognize and to spell out the implications of human finitude. To the extent that much interpretation of Kant has apparently lost sight of what I put forth as the controlling context of Kant's critical enterprise—the recognition of human finitude—my account of Kant will appear odd; conversely, to the extent that the recognition of human finitude is central to Kant's enterprise, there are few, if any, places more appropriate from which to start an inquiry that aptly can be termed moral theology.

There is, of course, an important connection between my use of a Kantian starting point and my understanding of the term "moral theology." The meaning with which my account invests that term will, I hope, become relatively clear by the time the reader reaches the end of this work. Although I do not propose to define that term here—that would go counter to what the journey image of the title is intended to suggest—I do think it proper to note one point about my use of this term in order to prevent undue confusion. There are some few contexts in which I have used the term "moral theology" to refer to the academic discipline that, particularly as it appeared in seminary curricula in recent centuries, had as a primary aim the pastoral training of priests for the sacramental office of confessor. As such, its focus was frequently upon the discernment of sin and culpability. In most contexts, however, I have used this term to refer to an intellectual enterprise more general in scope, which has as its aim the delimitation of the full contours of Christian life as it is lived, both by individuals and by communities, in response to God's grace. In using "moral theology" in this way I am denoting an enterprise that—although presupposed in the pastoral training more commonly called "moral theology"—has not yet come, in my judgment at least, to an adequately determinate shape, particularly in relation to philosophical discussions of moral theory.

The final context which has shaped this work is the one I consider most important. It is the context of the men and women—the friends and the strangers, the colleagues and the students, the individuals and the communities—through whom and with whom I have learned, and continue to learn, about freedom, community, imagination, and hope. The explicit acknowledgment I make here of some who have made it possible for me to produce this particular work is a token of gratitude to all the others left unnamed.

My first acknowledgment must go to three of my teachers—

O. K. Bouwsma, Edmund Pincoffs, and Alexander Von Schoen-
born — each of whom communicated a dedication to philosophical inquiry that has served as an ideal for my own work. I owe
much to the friends, colleagues, and students who have encour-
aged and challenged me in the enterprise of thinking through
and writing this work. William Everett, Ronald Green, John
Langan, S. J., William Prior, Mary Rousseau, and Roland Teske,
S. J., are among those who, at various stages, put the kind of questions needed to get my thinking clear; for the obscurities that
remain, I accept full blame. My deepest debt of gratitude is due
to Stanley Hauerwas for the well-focused criticisms he made of
earlier drafts, for the confidence he has shown in the value of
this work, and, most of all, for the generous colleagueship and
friendship which have been manifest in the interest he has taken
in my work.

The initial draft of this book was written during a year in
which I was a visiting scholar at the Woodstock Theological Center in Washington, D.C. Robert Mitchell, S. J., and Gerard
Campbell, S. J., who have been Directors of the Center, the research fellows and associates of the Center, and Henry Bertels,
S. J., the librarian of the Woodstock Theological Library, all have
my special thanks for their assistance during that year. My thanks
are also due to Robert Gassert, S. J., former dean of the College
of Liberal Arts at Marquette University, and William Kelly, S. J.,
chairman of the Theology Department, who approved my request for an academic leave to undertake this work; to Walter
Stohrer, S. J., rector, and to the Jesuit Community of Marquette
University, for financial support from the Jesuit Development
Fund and, most especially, for constant fraternal support in the
work of research, teaching, and writing; to the La Storta Jesuit
Community in Minneapolis and to the Jesuit School of Theology
at Berkeley for hospitality during summers in which I revised
the original manuscript; and to Camille Slowinski for her care
and patience in typing the various drafts of this work.

James Langford, director of the University of Notre Dame
Press, and Ann Rice, executive editor, have both been ever gracious and helpful in all matters connected with publication. William Jerman and Joseph Lienhard, S. J., have, in more than a
few places, saved me from falling into linguistic barbarity. I have
been most honored by the decision of the Publications Commit-

tee of the Catholic Theological Society of America to publish this work under its sponsorship.

My last, but surely not least, word of thanks is to Helen Mogck, who suggested the title of this work; in her friendship of many years I meet again and anew the reality of the hope toward which we all journey.

1. The Kingdom of God and the Kingdom of Ends

I. THE QUEST OF THEOLOGY

Freedom and the Tasks of Moral Theology

Among the classic descriptions of theology, there is one that has intriguing resonances for a philosopher: *fides quaerens intellectum* — faith on a quest for understanding. The main argument of this work surveys one area of human existence in which the believer's quest for understanding is pursued: human conduct and its moral governance. The point of the survey is to show that human conduct and its governance provide a suitable terrain upon which faith can hope to be successful in its quest for understanding.

There are a number of reasons whose convergence has impelled me to conduct this survey and to formulate the particular argument developed in chapters 2, 3, and 4. The most compelling ones arise from what I perceive to be ironically complementary failures on the part both of contemporary Catholic moral theology and of Anglo-American moral philosophy. Both enterprises have been less than successful in articulating a set of concepts that would enable us to understand human moral endeavor in its most fundamental terms: as the engagement of human freedom in the service of human mutuality — our likeness to, and dependence upon, one another. Contemporary Catholic moral theology has not been successful in articulating these concepts, because, in my judgment, it has lost confidence in the power

1

of philosophical concepts to disclose mutuality as a fundamental feature of human freedom. And contemporary Anglo-American philosophical ethics has been unable to articulate these concepts successfully, because, in my judgment, it has systematically evaded rendering an account of those features of human moral language and experience that can bring to light the ordering of human freedom to the service of mutuality.

The reasons for such failures are complex. The purpose of this work, however, is not to chronicle their sources and consequences; it is to present a case, stated in the categories of philosophical inquiry, for the reality that stands at the foundation of the enterprise of moral theology: human freedom in its essential ordering to human mutuality. This reality, it should be noted, does not constitute the whole foundation for moral theology. Human freedom, in fact, is able to stand as part of this foundation only in virtue of having its source in God's freedom. The relationship between human freedom and its source in God's freedom, however, is one that categories of philosophical inquiry can only indicate, but cannot explicate. Whatever explication we can make of this relationship is more properly a task for theological inquiry. This is so because theology, unlike philosophy, has its own essential purpose explicitly shaped by that relationship; theological inquiry is one element constituting the response of the freedom of a believing community to the initiative of God's freedom.

I am presenting a case for the role of human freedom at the foundation of moral theology because such an account is needed for moral theology to serve adequately its function within faith's quest for understanding: to point out to a Christian community, at each juncture and stage of its history, how faith illumines our efforts to understand human conduct and how such understanding, formed in faith, rightly enables our efforts to govern human conduct.

Why, then, is an account of the ordering of freedom to mutuality needed in order for moral theology to accomplish well this dual function of bringing the illumination of faith to bear upon our efforts to understand and to govern conduct rightly? It is needed because we cannot give a fully intelligible account of these efforts unless the postulate of the essential ordering of freedom to mutuality is shown to be true. We embark upon these efforts in consequence of freedom's bidding us to acknowledge our mutuality — that is, we seek to understand human conduct and to govern it rightly in virtue of a twofold recognition by what philosophers term our reason: that we are like to one another and that we venture into the future together. This recognition, however, would have no power to bring us to understand our conduct or to enable us to govern it rightly were it not itself an appeal to our freedom: we are each called upon to bring ourselves to see and to judge our conduct by reference to our likeness to one another. We are each called upon to allow our likeness to one another to be the fundamental basis for venturing into the future.

At the behest of our reason's recognition of our human mutuality, therefore, freedom empowers us to venture into the future. Essential to our venturing into the future is the enterprise of moral reflection: our best human efforts to understand and to govern rightly the conduct by which we go on together into the future. But these efforts have a limit placed on them: no matter how thorough our efforts to understand and to govern rightly our conduct, the future into which we venture does not take its shape solely in virtue of our conduct. It is the recognition of these limits — a recognition to be made in and by our freedom — that then allows us to place efforts to understand and to govern rightly our conduct within the ambit of faith — that is, to set ourselves to the tasks of moral theology. At these limits we are invited to acknowledge our need for imagination, which faith empowers, in order for us to see that what lies at the end of the path into the future is the completion of the reality whose recognition by reason bade freedom to set us on this path: our likeness to one another and our dependence upon one another.

Freedom and the Crisis of Surety

The connections among reason, freedom, and faith, which I indicated as setting the task of inquiry for moral theology, also suggest that one context in which the case I shall make for the ordering of freedom to mutuality might be set is that delimited by a task traditionally assigned to apologetics: showing the reasonableness of Christian faith. In fact the case I present contains elements that I think might be useful for constructing a "moral argument" for assent to, and trust in, the Christian God: the structure of our human moral existence, made manifest in the ordering of freedom to mutuality, is such that it is fully intelligible only as a sign inviting us to faith in a God who alone has the power to effect—now in sign and fully in the future—the abiding accomplishment of the mutuality to which freedom is ordered.

My main concern, however, is not apologetic. It is instead to lay bare the roots of some issues that I perceive to be indicative of a crisis besetting the moral thinking and practice of Christian communities in general, and the Roman Catholic community in particular. This crisis takes various guises and can be variously named. For Roman Catholics it is quite frequently seen as a crisis about the acceptance of the teaching authority of the church. I propose to speak of it, however, in terms that suggest that it is at least as much of a problem of moral epistemology as it is of church order and ecclesiology. It is a crisis that arises from the experience of being no longer able to find assurance adequate to enable us—be it as individuals or as a community—to sustain, intact and unambiguously, the set of moral beliefs and practices bequeathed to us from the past.

In the presence of such a crisis, moral theology, as an intellectual discipline, has appeared unable to accomplish adequately its function within the quest of faith for understanding. Although it once stood as itself a source of assurance for sustaining the moral beliefs and practices of the Roman Catholic community, it has now become for many a source of perplexity. For some it has even become a leading force in the undermining of cherished beliefs and practices. Roman Catholic moral theology appears to have become an enterprise on which we could aptly tag a catch phrase from the 1960s: no longer a solution, it has become part of the problem.

One reason, I suspect, why moral theology has become part of the problem is this: it did not itself attend to the enterprise of formulating a critically sound account of the foundation of its proper task and of its most basic concepts. It left to others the tasks of elaborating systematically and of showing the philosophical and theological adequacy of the sets of Aristotelian and Thomistic concepts and principles traditionally presupposed in the work of moral theology. Once, however, Catholic theologians and philosophers, engaged in the work of examining the conceptual foundations of their disciplines, began to explore seriously the possibility of formulating these foundations in terms other than those provided by the various traditions of Thomism, moral theology was left on its own for the work of elaborating its own foundations. That its own resources might not have been up to this work is suggested by two characteristics that have often marked efforts in recent Catholic moral theology to articulate its fundamental concepts: a philosophical eclecticism, which in one typical form, juxtaposes teleology and deontological moral theory with a "personalistic" anthropology, and efforts to use the theories and conclusions of the social sciences as a basis for formulating and confirming the significance of fundamental moral concepts.[1] Both efforts leave moral theology with little hope of establishing a philosophically adequate conceptual foundation for its work: the first effectively abandons central intellectual canons of consistency and coherence; the second ignores the problems that have beset philosophers and social and physical scientists in recent decades about the epistemic status and ontological significance of their concepts, principles, procedures, and theories.

The consequence of the incapacity of recent moral theology to render an adequate foundational account of its proper task and of its most basic concepts — which is of primary concern for this volume — is that moral theology has been rendered unable even to diagnose clearly, let alone prescribe appropriate remedies for, a mistake so deeply embedded in our contemporary self-understanding as to make it a fundamental source of the crisis about moral beliefs and practices that has gripped Christian communities. This mistake involves the way we conceive of our human freedom and the practices we have instituted to accord with that concept. The mistake is that we conceive of freedom primarily, if not exclusively, by reference to human agents in their individuality and independence, rather than in terms of their shared human communalities and their fundamental interdependence.[2]

The account I propose to give of the foundation for moral theology, therefore, will involve showing human freedom to be a power rooted as much in human communality and in interdependence as it is in human individuality and independence. It is my hope that such an account will enable us, as Christians, to formulate a needed challenge to our culture's understanding of freedom and its role in giving shape to human destiny. That understanding is one with which we are all familiar; it pictures human destiny coming more and more under conscious human control.

A challenge to this understanding also seems needed for us who profess to be Christians inasmuch as we too have come to accept this picture of human freedom and have used it to give shape to our interpretations of Christian belief and to the forms of our Christian practices. Though one now rarely hears discussion of the "death of God" theology that caught the fancy of headline-writers two decades ago, one of the main themes of that movement has become a commonplace of the theology of major Christian churches of the West, and has served to focus much reform and renewal of church practices: the mission of salvation has been entrusted into human hands. For the reflective enterprises of moral theology in the Roman Catholic tradition, and of Christian ethics in various Protestant traditions, this theme has been specified in terms of such concepts as responsibility, rights, the moral virtue of prudence, participation, collegiality, and — more ambitiously and ambiguously — liberation.

The task of challenging the depiction of human freedom that lies behind this theme and these concepts is particularly difficult because the reason the depiction is mistaken and misleading is not that it is wholly false; it is rather that, although true, it is not the whole truth, or, for that matter, the most important truth about the shape of human destiny. More important is a truth that faith proposes and to which reason can assent: our destiny, and the empowering of our freedom to work at its attainment, both come and require acknowledgment not as realities that are ours to control, but as gifts entrusted to our care.

It may very well be the case that this is the truth whose establishment is most important for the successful outcome of this foundational enterprise. It is a truth that, in my judgment, enables us to see fundamental connections between the power to shape our human moral conduct, which philosophers since Kant have characterized as moral autonomy, and the empowerment of our minds to see and our hearts to acknowledge the gift of our human destiny. This empowerment is a consequence of that relationship theologians call faith, which God enables us to have with himself. I shall speak of the former as the freedom of human moral endeavor and of the latter as the freedom of faith. I shall do so even though to many the latter seems quite unlike the freedom we exercise in moral endeavor. The freedom of faith is not of our own accomplishment; it is a freedom of receptivity, of the acceptance of a gift. Nonetheless, in the context of the effort of theology to understand human conduct from within the ambit of faith, the empowerment I have termed the freedom of faith stands as counterpart and as complement to our human power to shape moral conduct. This is so because the empowerment to see our human destiny as gift, given us by the freedom of faith, makes it possible for us to acknowledge something unexpected at the inner core of our autonomy: its character as also sheer, undeserved gift.[3]

Freedom: The Foundational Task

Much will be said in the course of this volume about the freedom of human moral endeavor and the freedom of faith. An image that suggests their relationship in the quest of moral theology for an understanding of human conduct is that of the harmony of voices in concert. The establishment of the possibility that they can so be in concert, however, depends upon showing the truth of a philosophical thesis that is central to this foundational project, but can surely be controverted: the inherent ordering of human freedom to mutuality. The thesis grounds the possibility of placing the power of the freedom of moral endeavor in full concert with the empowerment of the freedom of faith. This is so because, as will be shown in detail later, the ordering of freedom to mutuality stands as a pledge of the human destiny whose abiding attainment comes only as gift. This thesis is sure to be controverted because it is generally not taken to be the case that we are required, either as a matter of conceptual analysis or as a matter of giving shape to our practice, to accord the mutuality of human existence a central function in the workings of human freedom.

Mutuality, in its most general sense, is the facet of human life that encompasses all our relationships as persons to each other. In its most concrete guise, mutuality exhibits itself as the particular facts of our human relatedness: being of this family, speaking this language, being within these social, economic, and political configurations with one's own people and in reference to other peoples. In this guise, mutuality often appears to function as a polar opposite to freedom in the shaping of human conduct. Concrete relationships of mutuality define our interdependence and place constraints upon the scope of our conduct in virtue of that interdependence. The scope of actions taken in accordance with considerations of mutuality seems to serve as a limit to freedom's shaping of action. This, as we often, and quite unreflectively, conceive it, is the inherent spontaneity of human personal existence, made concrete and actual in the exercise of choice.[4]

The thesis that freedom is ordered to the service of mutuality offers one way to challenge accustomed ways of thinking of the mutuality of human existence as a limiting factor upon the exercise of human freedom. In establishing this thesis I hope to provide an account of human freedom in which its inner character of mutuality becomes manifest. We may then be able to see more accurately and, in consequence, bring into question our picturing of the relationship between human freedom and human mutuality as one of opposition. This opposition, moreover, has become embedded in practices we take to be paradigmatic of the exercise of human freedom and of the forms of human mutuality. It has also helped to shape the reflective analyses of human conduct characteristic of contemporary moral theory, in both its philosophical and theological expressions.

Freedom, Friendship, and the Constraints of Mutuality

The fact that we quite ordinarily presuppose freedom and mutuality to be in opposition to each other has become clear to me each time I have asked students, as part of their introduction to the study of ethics, to do some thinking about friendship. I ask them to do this as part of an initial consideration of human freedom. They generally find unobjectionable two premises I propose as a background for their thinking about friendship: (1) freedom is a power or capacity to choose; (2) an important kind (or exercise) of freedom is that of being able to choose your own friends. The thinking I then ask them to do is this: consider the way the friendships you value most have developed; see if you can locate any point in their history at which you chose Steve, or Sue, or Tom, or Terri, to be your friend or in which they chose you.

They find it hard to locate such a point for the simple reason that it is just not there: friendship emerges from choices, no doubt, but usually not from the explicitly formed choice to be a friend. When they pursue this line of thinking a bit further, they also begin to see that the crucial exercise of freedom in friendship often has to do, not with its initiation, but with its continuation and growth. They also begin to see that what continuation and growth often demand seems quite counter to the premise about freedom as the power of choice from which I asked them to start. The demands of friendship — a human relationship that we cherish as a fundamental locus of our freedom — constrain our power to choose, yet we consider ourselves no less free for all that. Once we have committed ourselves to being friends, we have no choice about the most basic matters that will sustain us in friendship — that is, we must be honest with each other, sensitive to the concerns of each other, available to help one another. Otherwise, the friendship will cease.

From giving this exercise to students, I have learned that even a brief reflection upon the complex role that freedom takes in the human reality of friendship serves to suggest a different way of picturing how freedom and our interdependence bear upon one another. The formulation of this mutual bearing initially sounds paradoxical — no doubt because we so readily assume freedom to have its ground in the individuality and independence of singular human agents. Reflection upon friendship suggests that, though the interdependence established and nurtured in friendship constrains choice, it gives depth to freedom by showing it to be the sustaining power of commitment as well as the momentary power of choice. This suggestion I shall later expand into a thesis that sounds even more paradoxical: human freedom has its most fundamental ground in the reality of our interdependence.

This exercise of reflecting upon friendship can help make us aware of the disturbingly ironic mistake in our self-understanding of freedom that has given shape to much contemporary moral theory and practice. For instance, moral philosophy, in many of its contemporary forms, has viewed moral life as an effort to sustain a maximal range of human choice within those constraints of mutuality that can be represented as universal. Such constraints may be thought of as requirements of reason.[5] According to this view, the ultimate ground for the moral character of human conduct lies in freedom. Though the ordinary forms of moral existence involve efforts to bring freedom and mutuality — as the latter is exhibited in the constraints of reason — into a working harmony, the possibility must be left open for freedom to stand its ground over against human understanding and reason. Without this possibility, the moral character of human existence would become a sham. The irony of this view is that even though mutuality provides conditions for the exercise of freedom to govern conduct morally, its constraints remain, nonetheless, the most potent threat to freedom. Freedom's last line of defense against the threat that mutuality can pose is to stand alone as the ultimate moral ground, even against those requirements of reason in which mutuality has been embodied.

Another exercise I ask students to do manifests the hold that this particular consequence of the common picturing of the opposition of mutuality to freedom has upon us. A preliminary to this exercise is a reading of the chapter "The Grand Inquisitor," from Dostoevski's *The Brothers Karamazov*. The chapter baffles many. As a help to seeing the issues it poses, I ask students to name a person, or persons, whom they consider to be most, or truly, free. Inevitably, the figure of "the hermit" is offered as a prime candidate for "most free." No wonder: it is the hermit who has most dramatically rejected what we have been bewitched to see as the most fundamental threat to our freedom — the fact that our lives are tied to one another. The lesson I draw from the results of this exercise is that the hermit represents well the stand against mutuality that modern moral theory judges freedom must be ready to take if it is to keep its moral power intact.

Moral theology, particularly when it has become preoccupied with the fashioning of finely detailed concrete norms for the governance of conduct, can also find itself setting mutuality in opposition to freedom.[6] In this preoccupation it can neglect to make explicit that the effort of faith to place human conduct in the service of mutuality has freedom as its very core. Moral theology enables us to identify the church as the concrete locus of mutuality for Christians. The church, therefore, has the responsibility to give shape to our freedom by reference to the forms mutuality takes within it, in order to place our understanding of human conduct and its governance concretely within the ambit of faith.

If, however, moral theology neglects to place the fundamental Christian mutuality that is church as the completion of the freedom exhibited in human moral endeavor, the result can be the perception that human freedom stands as an ever-possible threat to Christian mutuality. Like moral philosophy, moral theology will affirm that moral existence ordinarily requires the harmonious working of freedom in the context of mutuality. Unlike moral philosophy, however, it will, if need be, make the mutuality to which the church has been called the ground on which to take a stand over against human freedom. Christian mutuality must have a last line of defense against the threat that the freedom of moral endeavor, and the understanding that issues from it, can pose. This last line of defense is to take its stand as itself the ultimate moral ground. On this ground it may enlist allies: Scripture, tradition, and reason itself. When it so stands, it provides the mirror image of the irony of moral philosophy: there freedom must always have ground ready on which to take its stand against mutuality; here mutuality must always have ground ready on which to take its stand against freedom.

Because the church is the concrete, historical locus of mutuality for Christians, and because that mutuality is seen as grounded in God's unconditional call to establish a people as his own, Christians will always be subject to the temptation to use the concrete forms that mutuality takes in their particular communities as the last line of defense against claims made in the name of freedom, even by those whose will is to share in that community's mutuality. The Roman Catholic Church may very well be in the midst of a deep struggle with this temptation. The form the temptation takes is the enticingly simple view that the turmoil the church has experienced in the past two decades is, at root, a struggle between the opposing and irreconcilable forces of authority and dissent.

This is a view whose clarity is cherished both by "right" and by "left." It enables both of them to require those who do not see things so clearly to choose sides: infallible magisterium over against the clear errors of willful theologians; the myriad voices of those who experience the good of freedom over against the rigid and oppressive forms of doctrine and absolute moral principles. It is a view that places great stock in certainty, though the locus of certainty is variously conceived. On the one side it is in the formulations of magisterial pronouncements; on the other it is in the direct experience of freedom. Because this view places great stock in certainty, it is enticing when one considers the uncertainties that have beset Catholics — lay, clerical, and religious—for almost two decades. It is a view, however, that remains stubbornly blind to a far more prosaic view of uncertainty — that it is a condition we cannot avoid if we hope to learn anything about ourselves, our world, and our God.[7] On this account we can entertain the possibility that the uncertainties that have beset and continue to beset Catholics may simply be a prelude to the emergence of a fresh, though still recognizably and distinctively Catholic understanding of Christian mutuality, which will enable Catholics to renew the concrete forms of their church's life and practice.

The irony of the positions in which contemporary moral philosophy and moral theology have placed themselves is that most moral matters do not require us to take a stand on freedom as opposed to mutuality or on experience as opposed to authority — or vice versa. These reflective enterprises have placed themselves in the curious position of making a paradigm of moral experience out of an opposition that frequently is not manifest to one who makes the effort to lead a moral life. It seems that these disciplines hold fast to this opposition because we have almost all come to accept a picture of freedom modeled upon the exercise of individual choice.[8] As a result, we shape our reflective accounts of moral endeavor in ways that cannot but mislead us, because they place freedom and mutuality in opposition to one another at the very foundation of moral life.

Mutuality: Freedom in the Public Realm

I do not think it too great an oversimplification to say that many of the moods and moves both of contemporary moral philosophy and of moral theology are cast against this background: an ambiguous relationship between human mutuality and human freedom that finds them pitted against each other when serious moral matters are at stake. Against such a background, our quest for understanding — especially for an understanding with a capacity to govern conduct — can seem a parlous enterprise. Particular forms of this quest may be, from the very start, enlistments on one or the other side. Thus we may find ourselves entered upon the side of freedom or the side of mutuality without a clear perception of how it came to be: we entered once we started to govern our conduct in accord with the understanding offered by a particular form of this quest.

As long as we are willing to let the quest for an understanding of human conduct — be it a theological or a philosophical one — play itself out against such a background, the enterprises of moral philosophy and of moral theology will be powerless to bring such a quest to a satisfying conclusion. Against such a background one may even call into question the worth of a quest for understanding human conduct. Such a quest, in virtue of the context in which it must be conducted, cannot hope to rise above the ambiguities of mutuality and of freedom, if it at all remains faithful to the lived participation in these ambiguities by the ones who are questing.

There is, however, another background against which this quest may be pursued. It is the background suggested by images of the *public realm*, — commonwealth and kingdom, world and covenant, — that have had a long history in the enterprises of moral philosophy and of theology. They are images that we tend to interpret today in terms of the ambiguity of the relationship between freedom and mutuality. I hope to show, by the end of this work, that we should go at this the other way: *images of the public realm provide us with the power to see the fundamental inner connection between freedom and mutuality.* It is this inner connection that is at the foundation of moral living and of moral understanding. It is this inner connection that renders moral living and moral understanding open to transformation by and into the mutuality and the freedom of Christian faith, which has its origin in a transcendent and redeeming God.[9]

II. COMMONWEALTH AND KINGDOM: IMAGES OF THE MUTUALITY OF FREEDOM

The Public Realm and the Rationality of Choice

It may seem singularly unphilosophical to propose, as I have just done, to use an image, or types of images, to articulate the relationship and the inner connection between human freedom and human mutuality. Philosophical procedures, we might suppose, are the ones we employ to do precisely the opposite: to articulate a concept or a set of conceptual relationships, no matter what particular images or pictures we may ordinarily presume to provide the interpretive frame for our experience. In the case of freedom, for instance, the proper philosophical procedure seems to require that we articulate an understanding of freedom that is not dependent upon any particular images we may have of the shape of the public realm. If we cannot articulate an understanding with such independence from pictures of the public realm, we must try to specify its dependence only in terms of those features that are sufficiently general to be part of any public realm.

A good contemporary instance of the employment of this philosophical procedure is John Rawls's construction of the "original position" from which rational agents, armed only with the knowledge of certain general facts, make a choice of principles for the just governance of any public realm. Their freedom (which Rawls makes clear is of an ideal type) is conceived as one of rational choice; it operates upon the selection of a most fundamental set of moral principles — those that delimit justice — prior to any effort to give concrete shape to the public realm.[10]

Rawls tries to make the description of the original position independent of particular images of the public realm. There is, however, one element of his description for which this cannot be done: the notion of freedom exercised as rational choice. As Rawls explicates the notion of rational choice, particularly under what he terms "the Kantian interpretation," there clearly is a particular image of the public realm that gives substance to his explication. The image is that of free and equal legislative citizenship. This image is guiding in the sense that the choice of principles of justice can be judged to be "rational" and, thereby, a paradigmatic exercise of human freedom, in virtue of those features that constitute each person participating in the choice a member of an "ethical commonwealth." These features constitute a public realm such that the choice of principles is pictured, in an austere and idealized form of legislative procedure, as the outcome of a deliberation in which there is both equal voice and unanimity of consent. Human freedom in this public

realm is not primarily the inherent spontaneity of personal existence; it is the considered option for just those principles that
emerge from the conditions of equal voice and unanimity of consent, which constitute both this kind of public realm and oneself
as a member of it. [11]

The Moral World: The Context of Mutuality

The point of my discussion of Rawls is not to offer a criticism
of his procedure as inadequate; it is rather to point out that at
the heart of his procedure, though not always clearly articulated,
is a reliance upon a guiding image of the public realm and of
each person's power to play a founding role in that realm. I have
formulated the principal argument of this work in order to show
that we should pay careful attention to such images because they
guide our understanding of freedom and mutuality. These images deserve our attention because they can make manifest the
understanding of freedom that we place at the foundation of the
quest of moral theology. They make it manifest because they
enable us to represent the exercise of freedom at a level that is
different from and perhaps more fundamental than that so carefully explored by a thinker such as Rawls. I shall argue that the
images that are most appropriate for founding the quest of moral
theology are those that enable us to represent the exercise of
freedom not simply as a power of choice, but as a fundamental
human craving. I hope that my argument will make it plain that
there are images that enable us to represent the most fundamental exercise of human freedom as the acknowledgment of our
likeness to each other. These images thereby allow us to envision
human freedom and human mutuality as the mutual completion of each other.

These images are articulated out of the human experience of
freedom and of mutuality. But we do not enter into that experience apart from a context in which it takes definite shape. My
argument, therefore, aims to mark off contexts in which the exercise of our human freedom shows it to be ordered to mutuality. This involves spelling out the fundamental elements involved
in fashioning an image of a public realm for our action—that
is, our envisioning a moral world and our participation in it.
Within this context, the images by which we represent freedom

and mutuality function to give us our location with respect to one another as members and agents in that world.

The Moral World: Its Truth, Its Reality

Not every "world" we are able to envision can function as a moral world; nor is every moral world we envision one that enables freedom and mutuality to complement each other. These are two reasons why, in delimiting the context that shows freedom to be ordered to mutuality, we must confront questions about the possibility and the legitimacy of terming this context "true" and "real." Chapter 2 confronts these questions and thus advances claims about the truth and the reality of a moral world. These claims are based upon what our moral endeavor shows us to be the proper character of a moral world: a context for exercising our freedom in its ordering to mutuality, which "intersects" with our moral endeavor most fundamentally as a pledge and promise for the future. The moral world is pledge and promise of the future inasmuch as it is the realm of what ought to be, which nonetheless has power to give shape to our conduct. The power the moral world has to shape our conduct accounts for the way we have access to this world in its form as pledge and promise — that is, in the expectations we form for the moral future. These expectations express our hope for the outcome of our conduct.

Questions about the legitimacy of terming "true" and "real" a moral world that shows the exercise of freedom to be ordered to mutuality are not all answered simply by specifying its form to be pledge and promise. Claims of truth and reality advanced on behalf of a moral world must also bear upon the content of what is promised. Chapter 2, therefore, seeks also to make plain how our very efforts to represent a moral world disclose that the content of this pledge — the content of what is true and real in a moral world — is the fulness of human community.

Although the question of what is true and real in a moral world — its form, its content, and our manner of access to it — must be posed, for purposes of my foundational argument, in a singularly abstract and formal manner, at stake in the answer are matters far from abstract. At stake in the answer is the manner in which we are to lead our lives and to expect their completion. If I hope to provide a satisfactory answer in this work to the questions about the truth and the reality of a moral world, there must be a way to connect such an abstractly posed foundational question with the concrete stake our manner of living has in the truth of a specific moral world. The connection I propose, in chapter 2, lies in those narratives that show freedom setting us on the path to the completion of mutuality and thereby sustain us through time in a public realm of moral endeavor.[12]

There is more than one way to develop connections between narrative and what is true of a moral world. One way is to make a claim about narrative as a vehicle for conveying moral truth: narrative is the appropriate form for concretely presenting us with what is true of a moral world. This claim, however, is not sufficient for establishing the truth that philosophers such as Aristotle, or Plato, or Kant would claim for the moral worlds represented by their theories; neither is it sufficient for establishing the truth that Christian moral theology must claim for the moral world it affirms. These claims are not just about what is true of a moral world: they are claims that what is represented is the true moral world. This claim about narrative as the appropriate form for presenting what is true of a moral world is not sufficient to establish these strong philosophical and theological claims, because it does not provide us with any norm by which to assess the vastly different and conflicting moral worlds into which narrative can place us. The *Iliad* places us into a moral world, but it is a world in which the measure of human conduct is far different from that found in the world into which Sartre's *No Exit* places us. If we recount the life of Dorothy Day, we place ourselves in a moral world that is different in still another way. If we follow the career of Michael Corleone in the *Godfather* series, we enter into yet a fourth moral world. No matter how many or how few are the moral worlds into which narrative draws us, the formal claim made on behalf of the aptness of narrative as a vehicle for truth offers us no sure place from within these worlds by which we could affirm, with any legitimacy, the truth of one world over against the others. If we wish to determine such truth, we should have to appeal to a norm that in an important sense stands outside the particularities of each and every one of these narratives, and for which the narrative is thus only an illustration. Moral theory — be it Platonic, Kantian, utilitarian, contractarian, and the like — seeks to function as a norm of this kind. More informally, appeals we make to "the way it's always been done" (custom), or to "the way it is" (nature), to law, or to reason, can also be efforts to refer to a norm not tied to the particularities of circumstance that narrative must perforce exhibit even as it illustrates the norm.

Were moral theology just another form of moral theory, then leaving the connection between narrative and the truth of a moral world as that of illustration would be unproblematic. It would place whatever claims moral theory makes to truth under an adjudication made in accord with canons established to measure the adequacy of theories. However, inasmuch as there seems to be no agreement on how such canons apply to moral theory, the claims to truth made by moral theology — or by any other moral theory — must remain unresolved and perhaps unresolvable.[13] Moral theology — particularly in view of the function it has within the quest of faith for understanding — is, nonetheless, not just another form of moral theory. What it is, moreover, is dependent upon particularities in a way that suggests a need for a different, and far stronger, connection between narrative and the truth of a moral world. The particularities upon which moral theology depends are those that constitute the history of God's dealing with his people and, even more pointedly, the person who is Jesus Christ. Moral theology remains moral theory if all we are allowed to claim about Jesus Christ is that he is an illustration — albeit the perfect one — of God's love and freedom. Christian faith has usually claimed far more: that in Jesus there is, and that Jesus himself is, the full and definitive reality of God's love and freedom.

Particularity and the Truth of a Moral World

Christian faith makes the claim that the full and definitive reality of God's love and freedom is found in the particularity of Jesus Christ. This claim has consequences that provide a basis for characterizing, in a way appropriate for the work of moral theology, a relationship between narrative and the truth of a moral world that is far stronger than that of illustration. An important aspect of that relationship can be put thus: in order for a narrative to place us in a moral world that is true, it must enable us to see truth in and of the particularities it recounts. It must also enable us to cast our own lives as a narrative in which we can identify with those particularities in their truth, even while remaining in the truth of our own particularities.

There is a curious, even scandalous, incident in the Gospel of Mark that may help to illumine this point. It is the account (7:24–30) of the cure of the possessed child of a Syrophoenician woman. What appears scandalous about the incident is Jesus' initial response to the woman's request: he casts it in terms that underline how deep are the differences in particularity between Jew and Gentile: they are the differences between children and dogs, and these differences are sufficient to imply rejection of her request. Yet the woman, in her response, boldly identifies herself with the particularities Jesus' saying offered. In doing so, she heightens as well the particularity of her need and desire that her child be healed. The incident has a point and a poignancy that we might miss if, in our recalling and recounting of it, we fail to identify with the struggle of particularities it portrays: Jesus, in his particularity as Jew, as herald of God's reign, as healer, encounters this woman in her particularity, as Gentile, as one to whom the good news of God's reign need not yet be addressed, as mother of a possessed child.

We could, upon reflection on this incident, characterize moral theology as the effort of a Christian community, in the course of time, to understand the consequences for conduct that ensue from the encounters of our particularities, both as individuals and as a community, with the particularities of Jesus Christ. Central to this effort are recountings of these encounters — most importantly, those crystalized in the memory of the community — be they as brief as the incident of the Syrophoenician woman, or as extended as the whole of Scripture itself. These narratives are not simply illustrative of truth, though they are reduced to that when we do moral theology merely as moral theory. They are, more centrally, tales told so that from the truth of these encounters of particularities with the particularity of God's presence in Jesus Christ, the truth of our own encounters with his particularity can be brought to light and to life.

There is a second aspect of this stronger relationship between narrative and the truth of a moral world we should note now. This aspect can be termed narrative's empowering of our going on together. Because the truth central to the enterprise of moral

theology is shown — by narratives such as that of the Syrophoenician woman — to be bound to particularities, the going on together empowered by narrative must bear upon the truth of
particularities as well.

This point can be illustrated in terms of a challenge that has
begun explicitly to confront the efforts of Christian communities
to understand and to govern conduct rightly. This challenge arises
from the changes that have taken place in recent decades in our
awareness of the factors shaping our particularities as male and
female. These changes have made it clear that many of the
understandings and practices that once made it possible to go
together as male and female — in friendship, in marriage, as
members of God's people — can no longer do it well, or even at
all. In addition, we have not yet learned as best we can what
understandings are possible for us and what practices we must
now fashion to enable us to go on together. We may well be run-
ning risks of finding ourselves on paths that will make us go on
separately.

In the efforts of Christian communities to meet this challenge,
there is a central role that narrative is called to play. Narrative
is called to this role in virtue of the truth it can manifest to us
about the mutuality to which the exercise of our freedom is ordered: in narrative we can recount the possibilities of our going
on together. What Christian communities need, in order to meet
this challenge, are tales — old ones, new ones, even refashioned
ones — that recount a going on together that, in full awareness
of the differences of particularities, and indeed with a rejoicing
in them, is nonetheless abiding. Perhaps we have not yet recounted fully the narratives of the apostolic age, when a tale told
again and again was that Jew and Gentile, slave and free, male
and female, are all called together to abide as God's people.

The third and final aspect of the connection between narrative
and the truth of a moral world to be considered here is the function of narrative in establishing and sustaining images of the public realm. We need not turn to specifically Christian tales and
sources in order to see narrative functioning this way: we may
find its paradigm in Plato's *Republic*, and a modern, attenuated
instance in Rawls's *A Theory of Justice*. Plato most explicitly requires the telling of tales for the public realm of justice to take
hold, though he recognizes that ultimately they are insufficient

to sustain that realm enduringly.[14] Rawls's "original position" is a moral tale in the modern guise of a formal theory: it is the tale of how the rational being within us, if placed in the ideal circumstances of choice, would go about the task of selecting principles for living in a society of others who have set themselves to the same task.

The fact that, from the perspective of Rawls's theory, there is no reason to think of the original position as a narrative at all, let alone as a narrative more basic than the theory, points out something ironic in regard to this function of narrative: it can be done too successfully. We can come to think of the images of the public realm as having a life of their own, apart from the narratives that reveal their origin in efforts to sustain our human going on together. We find ourselves in this latter part of the twentieth century employing images of the public realm — or concepts derived from them — to guide our conduct long after we have ceased to have a need to retell, or to take seriously when retold, the narratives that recount their establishment. Once, however, images of the public realm are cut loose from the narratives that have established and sustained them, it becomes increasingly difficult for us to see why it is that we are all to go on together and how our particularities are to enable such going on together. We find ourselves in a public realm that has become a shell and is very easily shattered, again and again.[15]

The connection between narrative and the truth of a moral world whose aspects I have briefly delimited — the threefold power of narrative to exhibit the truth of our particularities as they encounter one another and the particularity of God's love and freedom in Jesus Christ; to enable us to go on together in and through our particularities; and to establish and to sustain for us images of a public realm — will be elaborated in more detail in the course of the argument presented in chapters 2, 3, and 4. They will then serve as the basis for a consideration of some issues that have taken their peculiar contemporary form in large measure because we have allowed the public realm to be shattered by our neglect of those possibilities for going on together that can best be sustained by narratives of the particularity of God's love and freedom shown in Jesus Christ. These issues will be considered in detail in chapter 5; I wish to take note of them in a preliminary fashion now, however, by delimiting the concrete moral concerns from which the elements of my argument issue. Notice of these concerns will, I hope, provide a clue to what might otherwise appear as rather arcane turns of the argument.

Two of the principal concerns that motivate my effort to place the foundations for human moral existence in the ordering of freedom to mutuality are (1) the loss of a public context for the moral continuity of our lives, and (2) the loss of confidence in imagination, particularly as it can be shaped through esthetic discipline, as a reliable path to public truth.

The Public Context: Moral Continuity

A public context for the moral continuity of our lives can be understood as that framework of moral principles and concepts that have been critically tested in time by the sustained efforts of a community to abide by them. Fashioning and sustaining such a public context is a complex matter; it requires a sensitivity to history, a critical stance toward the adequacy of one's own moral endeavor, a disposition to place one's moral evaluations under the considered scrutiny of other members of the community, and a willingness to essay a like scrutiny of the moral evaluations of others. The weakening or the loss of such a public context can come about as a result of the inability or even the unwillingness of the members of the community to engage themselves in one or another of the practices that sustain it.

The contemporary loss of a public context for the moral continuity of our lives instances, in my judgment, at least the inability to recount well and to heed the kind of narratives by which we can locate ourselves and our moral community in history. We can too easily forget the matrix of human experience out of which particular moral concepts were forged and too readily rely, instead, upon the public opinion pollster's sampling of the moral "climate," which, on controverted issues, can be as variable as the month of May along the Great Lakes. One large area of human living that has been placed under enormous stress by loss of a public context for the moral continuity of our lives can be found in the practices of marriage and family life. It does not seem too farfetched to claim that socio-economic factors reshaping these practices in directions that are morally problematic have been aided in doing so by the loss of a public sense of the common human temporality that makes fidelity a morally significant achievement.[16]

The initial stages of my argument address this kind of loss, though in an abstract mode, by elaborating the concepts — particularly imagination and narrative — that enable us to attend properly to the temporal dimensions of moral endeavor. Attention to these dimensions is important because they place the exercise of our freedom into the contexts that make manifest its ordering to mutuality.

The Public Context: Moral Continuity and the Common Good

There is a second instance of the loss of a public context for the moral continuity of our lives that suggests that there has also been an inability to engage in the kind of critical self-scrutiny and measured public discussion that sustains the public context. This second instance is the seeming impossibility of framing a notion of "common good" that can have a shaping impact upon the direction of public policy in a democratic polity. The price we have paid for the discovery that the terms expressive of the common good that had been enshrined as democratic ideals — life, liberty, and the pursuit of happiness — have their origins in the social location and economic interests of particular classes has been to declare, at least in practice, the bankruptcy of all efforts to speak of a good that is something more than a congeries of particular interests. We have lost confidence in the conviction that what has its origin in particularity can be fashioned through time to sustain the good of all.[17]

There are surely grounds for a suspicion of glibly formulated appeals to notions of "common good," particularly when they are employed to justify policies that stifle the efforts — be it of individuals or of groups — to locate themselves with their proper dignity in the human community. These need not, however, also be grounds for despairing of the possibility that we can fashion a notion of a good that is truly common — that is, shareable by each and all simply in virtue of membership in the polity and in the human community. The ground of such despair does not lie simply in demythologizations that unmask the deeply rooted particular interests at the heart of democratic ideals; it lies more

deeply in a failure of human imagination to seize upon the hints
of communality that can be found even in our deepest particularisms. Our human communalities — those features that make
it possible for us to say "I am as she; she is as I" — are particularly
fragile; yet they are the bases that must give us the confidence
to place our particularities in service to a common human good.

One point that I hope my argument supports is that imagination makes it possible to see our particularities giving strength
to our acknowledgment of human communalities as long as we
are willing to place those communalities in the public realm as
moral values and ideals. We cannot, however, impart strength
to our acknowledgment of communality, and thus to a common
good, if we continue to imagine (as certain developments in
economic and political practice apparently require us) our particularities to bear upon human communality only insofar as the
latter functions as a basis for settlement of the clash and clamor
of the interests we have in virtue of our particularities.

Communality conceived this way provides a realm that is public in an honorific sense at best: it allows all to participate in
the clash and clamor, but it excludes the possibility of a world
shared and shareable by each and all. Such "shareability" is, of
course, itself a human communality only hinted at in some of
our particularisms. It is a communality that nonetheless radically
constitutes us in moral existence if we have the imagination to
recognize it. It is a communality now not fully gained, but as
an ideal it empowers us to effect, at least in part, in the present
what it promises in fulness for the future. What I term "moral
imagination" in my argument can therefore also be thought of
as a human capacity for fashioning, out of our particularities,
a public context for our moral lives. It is precisely the capacity
to represent our human communalities as shared and shareable,
and our particularities as enabling interdependence, which constitutes the dynamisms of our moral endeavor to be not just a
harmonizing of particular interests but a common striving for
good. These communalities go by names such as dignity, human
nature, endeavor, feeling, and the like, and it is from them that
a moral world in which we can, in all our particularity, be interdependent, begins to take shape. Failure to shape a public
context for our moral lives in terms of concepts such as these can
be taken to be symptomatic of what we have to judge an even

more damaging failure: loss of confidence in imagination as a
reliable path to public truth.

The Public Context:
Worship and the Shape of Moral Imagination

We may gain a sense for this connection by considering, in
a preliminary fashion now, one realm of practice in which, as
chapter 5 will show in more detail, the loss of a public context
for the continuity of moral life has had a dramatic effect. This
is the realm constituted by the public worship of the church whose
traditions hold my allegiance and shape my life—the Roman
Catholic Church. This consideration will help show this connection because the practices of worship have played a particularly
important, though not always clearly acknowledged, role in shaping the images that delimit the public context of Catholic moral
life. The particular focus of my considerations here and in chapter
5 will be upon the function of these practices in providing for
those who participate in them the sense of living in a shared and
shareable world.

The tight interweaving of Catholic belief and practice with
particular ethnic heritages in the United States was probably
already in the process of unraveling even before the Second Vatican Council, chiefly as a result of forces moving Catholics willy-
nilly more and more into the curious homogeneity *cum* particularisms of American life. A prominent victim of these processes
has been the security of living in a shared world that was identifiably Catholic in its ways of thinking and of acting. Some of
the vicissitudes that have beset Catholicism in the United States
and elsewhere in the past two decades can be placed in clearer
focus, I believe, from the foundational perspective that my argument proposes. This perspective will enable us to locate in the
public worship of Christian communities a place in which are
told the narratives of the encounter of human particularity with
God's particularity, and, thus, a principal source for those images of the public realm that constitute a shared moral world
for Christians.[18] There is, consequently, little doubt in my mind
that the whole range of Catholic sacramental practice, as well
as the public forms of popular piety, have always been central
for setting the public context for the moral continuity of the lives

of Catholic Christians. I believe that a convincing case can be
made that the trauma of the apparent loss of a shared world that
is identifiably Catholic points to a fundamental moral dynamism
to be found in the realm of worship. As a result of this dynamism,
changes in the forms of Catholic worship, however gently made,
have signaled significant alterations in the public context that
is to shape the lives of Catholics and give those lives moral continuity. Some have, of course, perceived these changes more
radically — namely, that they provide a substantially different
public context for Catholic life.

Determining the extent to which the public context of Catholic
moral existence has been and will continue to be altered under the
impact of new forms of sacramental and paraliturgical practice is
not, I suspect, within the predictive powers of any of us. The
fact that there is a connection of this kind between public worship and moral life is of major importance, however, for my endeavor to provide an account of the foundation that the quest of
moral theology for understanding has in human freedom and human mutuality. The relationship between worship and moral life
is important because it provides a concrete locus for exhibiting the
empowerment of human imagination so that it may provide us
with pictures of the full shape and dimensions of the public realm.

Worship is not the only human activity in which imagination
can be invested with the power to present and to represent truth.
Chief among the other activities in which it can be so invested
are the ones we call the arts. Yet our contemporary culture deals
no more kindly with them than it does with worship when those
who participate in these activities take the concrete signs, symbols, and images of the arts to present and represent a truth that
is public. Our culture has schooled us well in this regard: we
do not expect someone to press claims to public truth in the name
of artistic imagination. When such a claim is pressed, as Solzhenitsyn has done, the kindest response it can hope to evoke is
sympathetic puzzlement.[19] The claim of worship is, of course,
even more quickly ruled out of court. My argument, nonetheless,
marks off the chief responsibilities of moral philosophy and moral
theology by reference to such activities. These disciplines serve
as reflective and critical moments in those human enterprises that
invest imagination with the power to present and to represent

moral truth in a public way. I pose this argument precisely with the intention of calling to mind how fundamental elements of the enterprise of moral living depend upon the exercise of imagination. We frame our actions out of a communality we glimpse only fitfully, and for a community whose full shape we can envision only for the future.

Imagination and the Moral Future

Chapter 3 will carry forward my argument that the foundation for moral theology is most appropriately disclosed in images of the public realm that enable us to see the inner connection of human freedom and human mutuality. We are able to frame our action out of a communality we glimpse only fitfully, and for a community whose full shape we can envision only for the future, in virtue of the central role that imagination plays at the foundation of our moral reasonings. The central role of imagination in moral reasoning has generally been given short shrift by philosophy. I shall propose, however, an account of this role, constructed on the basis of Kant's notion of "moral faith," which constitutes imagination as a principal juncture for the enterprises of moral philosophy and moral theology. The basis of this account will be the concepts of hope and of human destiny, as they function in Kant's depiction of human freedom.

These concepts make it possible for us to understand that central to imagination's function in human moral endeavor is the representation of human communality for the moral future. This representation takes form as an image of human moral destiny. The human comportment toward this representation that appropriately marks its significance for moral endeavor is then to be designated "hope."

Chapter 3 moves my argument forward by using this understanding of imagination to disclose how the freedom of human moral endeavor is rendered open to the freedom of faith. Before I outline its procedure, however, a brief mention of the principal concrete moral concern I see at stake at this stage of my argument can once again prove useful in gaining an overall sense for the argument. At stake is the certainty we are entitled to seek and to expect in moral matters.

Imagination and the Moral Future: Education for Justice

The certainty we may justifiably have in moral matters is a function of the manner by which we have access to what is true and real in the moral world. That access, in my argument, is most fundamentally provided for us by hope. The outcome of our efforts to effect and to sustain sureness in moral matters will be disappointed, therefore, when we fail to apprehend the reality and the truth of the moral world according to the form by which it is given us in hope. That form is one of pledge and promise. The practices that a community institutes, both formally and informally, for moral training and education constitute a major effort both to effect and to maintain certainty in moral matters. These practices, therefore, are particularly liable to show the marks of any failure to apprehend the reality and truth of the moral world according to its form, given by hope, of pledge and promise.

In view of this relationship between the sureness we can have in moral matters and hope as our manner of access to what is true and real in the moral world, it seems prudent to proceed with some caution in assessing the surge of interest that has developed in recent years for theories of moral development and for their potential application to the practices of moral education. The caution I urge is not intended to suggest that there are fundamental inadequacies in theories of moral development. It is intended, instead, to remind us of the need to bring to light and to examine critically whether the certainties we attempt to hand on to the next generation through the practices of moral education have their bases in a hope for the moral future in which we see a pledge of full human mutuality. We need to be especially careful that what we, as moral educators or as parents, unreflectively take to be moral certainties are not, in fact, in opposition to reflective and critical dynamisms focused upon the moral future that are necessary for every authentic practice of moral education. The thesis for which I argue in chapter 3 — that the function of hope in human moral endeavor is its empowerment of our imagination to represent the moral future as one of the completion of human communality and interdependence — is intended to suggest where to look for our most deeply cherished moral certainties so that we may then hold them up to critical

examination: they are located in the hopes we have for the final
and the lasting form our mutuality with others will take. They
are truly cherished to the extent that we allow these hopes to
give shape to the whole range of our conduct.

I single out moral education as an area to which the discussion of hope in chapter 3 is particularly pointed because I am
worried about the possibility that an especially pernicious form
of bad faith may infect expectations brought by educators and
parents to practices of education intended to foster moral growth.
I term it pernicious because it is a form of bad faith that would
require society's moral educators to adopt Socrates' method to
transmit the message of the sophists.

My worry can be put thus: if we take a theory of moral development, such as the one elaborated by Kohlberg, as a guide to
developing practices of moral education, then we must be willing, first, to envision the moral future in accord with that theory:
the final and lasting form of human mutuality is to be a society
that is just. We must then be willing to shape all our conduct
in accord with that vision. The justice of this society is not a Platonic social harmony; it is the fairness of persons and of struc-
tures in settling conflicts of interest that arise among persons to
whom equal respect is due. It is not evident to me, however, that
concerns for more effective moral education, as they have been
voiced in the United States, always or even often issue from hopes
for the moral future of a just society akin to the one envisioned
in Kohlberg's theory. Neither is it clear that the just society envisioned in Kohlberg's theory is adequate to represent, even partially, the hope for the completion of human mutuality founded
upon Christian faith.[20] Concern that sons and daughters be edu-
cated to become morally good persons can all too often have as
its sole focus the rectitude of personal moral conduct detached
from an effective concern for the public dimensions of our mutuality and interdependence. The possibility for fostering bad
faith arises when this reduced focus is taken to encompass the
moral world—that is, is not taken as part of a larger vision of
a just society. The practice of moral education in accord with
Kohlberg's theories requires that an understanding of one's personal conduct be placed within the context of learning how to
fashion and act upon a critical judgment in regard to the practice and promotion of justice in society. The same would be true

of practices of moral education formed in accord with the growing awareness in the Catholic Church, both in proclamation and in practice, that the promotion of justice in society is central to Christian moral responsibility both to God and to neighbor. These practices of moral education, therefore, gain their reflective and critical focus from the hope that the moral future ought to take form as a just society. This focus, however, can place the moral educator in an ambiguous position if that hope is rarely acknowledged elsewhere as a significant shaping element for conduct in society. In those circumstances, moral education that is effective for developing critical and reflective attitudes and motives for conduct based on such hope can even be perceived as a threat to the concern for fostering personal moral rectitude. Of necessity it relativizes that concern by placing it in a wider context governed by a concern for the promotion of justice in society.

Chapter 5 will discuss in more detail some of the ramifications of this dilemma. The point I wish to note now is that this dilemma can be shown to have its root in differing ways of portraying the moral future — ways that are a function of how we understand the relationship of freedom to mutuality. My effort in chapter 3 to indicate that hope requires that we bring our moral certainties to focus upon our portrayals of the moral future can therefore be understood to suggest one path for the resolution of this dilemma and others like it. That path requires that we have the courage both to articulate our representations of the moral future and to evaluate their adequacy for manifesting the hope that Christian faith calls us to have in the gift of human destiny.

Imagination and the Moral Future: The "Highest Good" and God's Transcendence

Our expectations for the moral future can therefore affect our moral existence concretely by giving shape to the practices of moral education. They can affect our moral existence even more profoundly if, as the continuation of my argument in chapters 3 and 4 will claim, they constitute a feature of the moral life that renders it open to transformation in response to God's transcendence. This stage of my argument will make use of an interpretation of Kant's account of the object of our expectations —

which he terms the "highest good" — to explicate the manner in which we are rendered open to transcendence.[21]

My reliance on Kant's account is dictated by the fact that his doctrine of the "highest good" can be articulated into a summary formulation of my main argument: human freedom, exercised in moral endeavor, gives rise to hope in such a form — that is, as an expectation about human destiny — that it can be brought to completion only in terms of human mutuality — that is, full and lasting participation in a public realm. By employing the doctrine of the "highest good" in a philosophical account of the foundations of moral theology, however, I am stepping beyond the bounds that Kant thought constrained such an enterprise. My justification for doing so rests upon the "logical space" that I perceive Kant's account nonetheless leaves for such a venture. This logical space is cleared by Kant's conviction of the finite character of human existence. The consequence of venturing into this logical space is that we are enabled to glimpse how freedom can be rendered open to God's transcendence in moral endeavor: the mutuality that brings our moral expectations to completion is constituted by participation in a public realm whose full accomplishment, for all our striving, lies beyond human endeavor. Although its possibility is within our power of representation — it is the commonwealth of reason — its actuality can be represented only as the outcome of gift — it is the kingdom of grace, represented by the human capacity most open to being gifted because it is most powerless: imagination.

Chapter 3 brings to a close the part of my argument that I judge to be most properly philosophical both in its manner of procedure and in regard to the realm of human existence of which it tries to render an account. There are a number of central points advanced in the course of my argument that I therefore deem adequately justifiable simply in virtue of their being accurate renderings of the features or conditions of human moral experience, whether or not one thinks that such experience is thereby made open to God's transcendence, to grace, or to faith. These points include the inherent ordering of human freedom to the service of mutuality, the fundamental role of imagination in our moral reasonings, and the pledge of moral community as the most fundamental form of the truth of morality.

Gift and Practice

In chapter 4, theological considerations, particularly those that show God's initiative at work in human mutuality, have an explicit function in the continuation of my argument. Chapter 4 is an effort to show how human moral experience can be rendered open to an understanding that issues from the freedom of faith: it is rendered open in consequence of the inherent connection between human freedom and human mutuality. As in previous chapters, there is a particular moral concern at work behind the abstract movements of my argument. The principal concern in chapter 4 is the rootedness of our human practices in the authentic mutuality of human freedom. The specific way that chapter 4 attempts to deal with this concern is by offering an account of the gifted character of our human cravings. In this account, the craving for mutuality is singled out as a paradigm of such "gifting." My hope is that an account of the gifted character of our cravings may serve as a reminder of the fundamental moral and religious significance of our need to rely upon one another for the enjoyment and satisfaction of our cravings. Its significance is that the finitude of our human freedom, which faith enables us to see as itself God's gift, evokes God's response of the further gift of a share in his own mutuality.

The other concerns that I have already noted to be at issue behind the movement of my argument can also be formulated in terms of this concern for the rootedness of our human practices in the mutuality of freedom. The loss of a public context for our moral lives, the loss of confidence in the power of esthetically disciplined imagination to disclose public truth, the search for moral surety without a clear awareness of the form of moral truth, are all signs that basic practices of human interaction at the core of our personal and social existence are being uprooted from their source in the mutuality of human freedom. This can often be seen in its most manifest forms in the particular areas I have already mentioned as my concrete focuses for these concerns.

Fidelity ceases to be a morally significant achievement for shaping a public sense for the reality of marriage and family life once the practices of marriage and family life cease, for whatever reason, to make it possible for the exercise of freedom to effect mutual trust and understanding. A notion of the common good becomes impossible to frame once the practices of socio-economic and political life are fashioned on the presumptions that the exercise of freedom functions only to foster particular interests, and that the particularity of interests is so fundamental that even when they are pursued jointly by many individuals their confluence is, at root, the fortuitous summation of arbitrary choices. Worship ceases to provide a community with the images and substance of a shared world once it is forgotten that we are called to worship so that God may empower a shared understanding and trust among us that is beyond the grasp of our own endeavor. Moral education can become — equally for parents, educators, and students — bad faith if the forces in society that shape the practices of education operate upon the basis of a picture of human interaction that portrays education simply as one of the instruments for fostering the pursuit of particular interests.

Gift and Practice: Profession as Service

Chapter 4 is not intended to suggest that there is an uncomplicated movement from an awareness of the gifted character of human cravings to a refashioning of human practices so that they disclose mutuality. It is intended to suggest, instead, that such an awareness can serve as a starting point from which we can then understand, assess, and move on to refound or refashion the practices that shape our lives as members of a public realm. Let one broadly sketched illustration suffice to highlight this point now; more will be said about it in chapter 5.

A growing number of specialized fields of human skill and endeavor have been undergoing processes that have been designated "professionalization." There are many complex human cravings and a whole range of interests, both of individuals and of groups, involved in these processes. This mixture makes for considerable moral ambiguity in the development of practices both to mark out individuals as members of a profession, and to place a particular profession itself in relation to other professions. It has not been uncommon in recent years for professionalization to be a source of disputes that have had a particularly bitter edge to them. Parties to such disputes can even go to seemingly scandalous lengths to establish or to protect professional "turf." Behind such conduct there may very well be, unreflectively assumed, a particular picture of the interplay of human cravings and interests: they are demands to be satisfied, some so insistent that their satisfaction must be accomplished even at the expense of human mutuality. In accord with this picture, conflict over cravings and interests is not only possible, it is inevitable. Norms for the resolution of such conflicts can be established, but they have as a condition for effectiveness the possibility of agreement upon a common interest of greater weight than the other particular interests at stake in a specific dispute. This condition obviously is not always met; sometimes it is met only enough to mute, rather than resolve, the conflict.

If, however, one reflectively adopts a picture of human cravings and interests as gifts to be rendered at the service of the human mutuality at the core of freedom, then there are different patterns possible both for understanding and for guiding the interplay of human cravings and interests. One can start to think of the mutuality at stake in the dynamics of professionalization as one that requires that the practices being fashioned be measured in terms of their suitability and effectiveness for making available throughout society at large, the skills and the knowledge of both extant and nascent professions. Conflict is by no means precluded, but it can be made more tractable if those who come into conflict retain a willingness to be reminded that a shared commitment to the service of mutuality serves in a most explicit way as norm for the guidance of conduct and the shaping of practices in those human activities that are properly termed professions.

Adoption of a picture of human cravings and interests as gifts to be rendered at the service of the human mutuality at the core of freedom should be done without closing one's eyes to the fact that the actual interplay of human cravings and interests has been tangled enough in most human endeavors to justify the metaphor we often apply in frustration to the marketplace, the workplace, and even to academia: "jungle." One should also be aware that adopting the picture of "gift" requires a radical shift in understanding the relationship one may now appropriately bear to one's own interests and cravings: they are no longer to be served uncritically, but are to be put in service for the mutual shaping and sharing of a world. Adopting this picture can aptly be termed a "conversion." It is a conversion that stands as a condition of possibility for retrieving or refashioning human practices so that they may disclose the mutuality to which the exercise of freedom in these practices is ordered.

An account of the gifted character of our human cravings not only provides a way for retrieving or refashioning human practices so that they disclose mutuality, it also brings to completion the argument for the reality of the moral world in which freedom is ordered to mutuality — an argument initiated in chapter 2. The completion of this argument, however, is not itself an argument; the completion of this argument is found in concrete narratives in which this world is imaged, in a definitive manner, as the pledge, promise, and power of the mutuality of human freedom. These are the narratives of our human efforts to utter an abiding "we." These are the narratives of God's invitation for us to utter an abiding "we" as his people. These are the narratives that Christian faith is able to identify as having their full and lasting disclosure in Jesus Christ.

Moral Theology:
The Freedom of Faith and Sacramental Imagination

Quite obviously, this completion is not one for which justification can be offered simply on philosophical grounds. Those grounds enable us only to render the elements of moral experience that point in the direction of its completion; they do not require us to cast off in that direction. They may even suggest that we are unable to cast off for and arrive successfully at that completion unless there first be a call to us from that direction. As a result, chapter 4 moves within the ambit of moral theology, inasmuch as the call from the direction to which our moral experience points us is what Christian understanding calls "faith." If we cast off in the direction to which faith calls us, then a new perspective is opened for the reflective enterprise of understanding human conduct. Human conduct is now to be understood from the perspective of the destiny to which we are called in faith. Whatever else this destiny involves, it surely involves mutuality: entrance into that mutuality of God's own life that Christian understanding designates "grace."

Chapter 4, therefore, concludes my argument by touching

upon one consequence of the relationship between the mutuality that calls upon the exercise of freedom in moral endeavor and the mutuality of God's life to which we are called in and through faith. This consequence is one I term the "transformation of reason," with which we first reflectively acknowledge our human likeness and interdependence. Reason is transformed into the imaginative power of the freedom of faith so that we may begin to comprehend the full significance of the images of the public realm. These images now help us to see that the mutuality at the core of human freedom is offered as an effective sign of the invitation to share in God's mutuality. This significance is one that I think can justly be termed "sacramental": these images have been gifted, by the power of the narrative word, with the power to effect the mutuality they promise.

My argument for the reality of the moral world, which started with moral imagination, thus comes to a close by leading us to the possibility of engaging our imagination in a way that can be appropriately termed "sacramental." Through sacramental imagination we are enabled to represent the full attainment of mutuality with one another and with God in its power to effect that mutuality in us, not for the moral future only, but here and now. The moral world is thus made most real in the order of grace.

2. Imagination and the Truth of Morality

I. THEORY WORLD AND STORY WORLD

Freedom: The Tale of Interdependence, The Tale of Self-Sufficiency

This chapter initiates an argument that will extend through chapters 3 and 4. I have already noted the chief point in support of which this argument is offered: the essential ordering of freedom to mutuality. I am presenting this argument even though I am convinced that one's most basic grounds for apprehending this point — or, for that matter, any other central philosophical or religious point — and for acknowledging its truth, rarely rest on arguments put forth by philosophers or theologians. I think that this is particularly true in this case, inasmuch as one of the main lines of my argument is that narrative — not argument — has the fundamental power to enable us to see and to acknowledge the truth of the ordering of our freedom to mutuality.

If narrative has the fundamental power to lead us to see this truth, what reasons are there for constructing an argument in its support? Would not a well-told tale do the job better? It probably would. So perhaps my fundamental reason for offering an argument is simply that I am not a good storyteller. There are, however, more positive and less autobiographical reasons I can offer, and I hope they will prove helpful for delimiting the overall shape and purpose of my argument, and for locating it in the context of some contemporary philosophical and theological discussions.

37

One reason — perhaps the most important in regard to those who do not yet see how freedom can have an essential ordering to mutuality — is that this argument, if it succeeds in highlighting some of the fundamental conceptual difficulties consequent upon severing freedom from mutuality, may urge us to go back to trace the roots of our convictions about freedom. If the argument provokes us to that task, it then may put us in a position from which it is possible to see that those roots are, most fundamentally, the stories and images that shape our understanding of who we are and our hopes about who we are to become.[1]

Our need to be provoked to trace the roots of our convictions about freedom may be suggested by considering again the kind of exercise I propose to students to help their critical thinking about freedom. These exercises are intended to bring them to identify some of the conceptual difficulties — which may then help them deal with the experienced difficulties — that follow from severing freedom from mutuality. I have found students to have a fundamental conviction — which they may not be able to express well in the abstract terms I shall use — that the power to be a friend and the capacity to be befriended are integral to that which identifies them as free. This conviction has its sources in the friendships that they are trying now to live and that they can be helped to articulate as narratives of the trials, successes, and failures of their learning the skills of going on with one another.

If their understanding of freedom were based simply on this conviction, its conceptual articulation would pose relatively few difficulties. There is, however, another narrative that also shapes their fundamental convictions about freedom. It is a narrative of independence and of self-sufficiency, which has its intellectual roots in the Enlightenment — though most students believe they thought it up all by themselves — and which gets reinforced by the congeries of items that in these latter years of the twentieth century seem to be the most prominent features of our public world: the political rhetoric, economic practices, psychological theories, media "hype," and the like, which promise ever-growing horizons of personal satisfaction.

This second narrative, significantly, is not as much their own as the first, particularly in their everyday dealings with one another. It is, nonetheless, though not surprisingly, more central than the first in their conceptual understanding of freedom: freedom is self-sufficiency. It is, in fact, the self-sufficiency most aptly exemplified by the one who has withdrawn from even the possibility of friendship: the hermit. The clash of these convictions can then be put in rather stark terms: if one is truly free, one must avoid taking on the entanglements of friendship. Most students rightly find this conclusion unsatisfying. They can, however, also recognize its logic, which then makes all the more frustrating the difficulties they frequently have articulating the reasons for their dissatisfaction. I then suggest to them that a shift in perspective might prove helpful: they should cease to worry about the limitations that friendship places on independence and on choice, and begin to consider, instead, what consequences follow from taking friendship, in all of its complexity, to provide a model of the workings and significance of freedom. The shift of perspective I suggest is, of course, to that of the ordering of freedom to mutuality. One item that affects their willingness to attempt such a shift is the extent to which the exercise has been successful in perplexing them with difficulties about the identification they presumed freedom to have with independence and self-sufficiency.

These exercises, and their results, form the pedagogical background against which my argument is cast. Against that background the argument of this work can be understood as an effort to present in more general conceptual terms the clash of convictions crystalized by such an exercise and then to articulate reasons for thinking that human interdependence, such as that taken on in friendship, provides the most adequate and fundamental basis for our thinking about freedom.

Another reason I have for constructing an extended argument for the ordering of freedom to mutuality is that freedom provides what may well be the most appropriate conceptual locus for reaffirming and for rethinking the long-standing confidence of Roman Catholic tradition in the congruence, compatibility, and cooperation of reason with faith. At the outset of chapter 1, I noted what I termed the loss of confidence of Roman Catholic moral theology in the power of philosophical concepts to disclose mutuality as a fundamental feature of human freedom. This loss of confidence is but one instance, though one of the most crucial, of far larger issues regarding the function of philosophy within the life of faith and for the reflective enterprise of theology in Roman Catholicism. A full statement of those issues is not within the purview of this volume. What I am offering is, instead, an account of concepts fundamental to moral life that I hope instances the kind of congruence, compatibility, and cooperation of reason with faith in which the Roman Catholic tradition has long professed confidence.[2]

More particularly, I have constructed this account as an argument that self-consciously moves from considerations that are offered on philosophical grounds to ones offered on theological grounds. The considerations that I propose on philosophical grounds are ones whose intelligibility and use for moral life do not require assent to specifically Christian beliefs. The recognition that we are like one another and that we venture into the future together are considerations of this kind. Although it may be the case that these considerations have taken a certain shape when they have functioned in the context of Christian faith and practice, the initial stages of my argument do not require reference to this context of Christian faith in order to show the significance these considerations have for the foundation of moral life. The considerations I then propose, on theological grounds, in the concluding stages of my argument build upon the considerations previously offered on philosophical grounds. Thus the hope in human destiny that has its basis in our recognition of human likeness and our need to journey on together into the future is shown to take its definitive shape in terms of the particular revelation of God that is found and enacted in Jesus Christ. This move from philosophical to theological considerations is made in the transition from chapter 3 to chapter 4. Two indices of this move are the turn made in chapter 4 to the language of gift and craving, and the eschatological perspective opened up for us by what that chapter discusses as the transformation of imagination.

An argument that attempts to move from philosophy to theology can be offered with apologetic intent; it can be addressed to those who can be presumed to share the main philosophical convictions from which the argument starts but who do not assent to the consequences that can be drawn from those convictions on the basis of Christian faith. Although I would be pleased if my argument did have the apologetic effect of aiding someone to assent to Christian faith, its effort to delimit a movement from philosophy to theology has not primarily been constructed with apologetics in mind. This particular feature of my argument — that is, its effort to instance the congruence of reason with faith — is principally addressed to those with whom I share Christian convictions but who may not see compelling reasons for providing these convictions, to the extent that it is possible, with a conceptual framework able to stand up under inspection made in accord with canons of philosophical adequacy. In setting forth my argument, therefore, I am somewhat less concerned with convincing readers of the correctness of the particular Kantian philosophical framework I have elaborated — though I should be pleased with that result — than I am with provoking them to comparable elaborations of the philosophical frameworks that function to aid faith in its quest for understanding.

I see a particular need for such efforts within the enterprise of Roman Catholic theology. Its confidence in the congruence of reason with faith, so long professedly tied to a commitment to the philosophical adequacy of an ideally conceived "Thomism," has become far more modest in the last two decades. There seems to be an acceptance of philosophical pluralism, at least as a "fact of life," in the intellectual training for serious students of theology. There are, as well, efforts to utilize systematically certain non-Thomistic frameworks, most notably those constructed from process or from dialectical categories. Yet most of this appears to have happened — particularly in the United States — in relative isolation from the concerns, arguments, and issues that preoccupy most of those who are trained and who train others in the discipline of philosophy. The pluralism of philosophical training was not planned, least of all as an effort to provide the basis for a long-term effort to rethink the conceptual foundations of Catholic theology. The interest in different conceptual frameworks was not confined to those provided by philosophy but extended to those offered by psychology and sociology. In consequence, for the enterprise of Catholic theology, philosophy has apparently now become one conceptual tool among many, and a tool that may even be judged less reliable than most.[3]

I do not take my argument to contain a remedy — either instant or long-term — for this situation. In showing far less confidence in philosophy than it once had, Catholic theology is, no doubt, also reflecting a deep-seated contemporary cultural distrust of reason, and especially of the most abstract forms of the use of reason. I am offering my argument in the hope that it can be an instance in which philosophy serves to sharpen the understanding that faith seeks, not by the happenstance of having, for the nonce, the particular concept useful for founding moral theology, but by reason of its requirement that our understanding subject itself to critical norms before it can offer us satisfaction that we have affirmed what is true.

My argument is constructed, therefore, to serve a variety of purposes, not all of which are explicitly contained in its conclusion. I am particularly concerned that it function to bring us to consider with care whether or not we have accurately located the fundamental import and purpose of the exercise of our freedom. I hope that my argument will help to show that its import and purpose are as much for others as for oneself. In consequence, we may then be able to discover that the primary context of our freedom is not, as our culture has accustomed us to think, the realm of what is private to each of us but, instead, the domain of what is public, the whole range of what we are called upon to see and to share with one another.

"The World": Locus for Truth

My argument begins, therefore, with a consideration of the concept we use when we speak in most general and most fundamental terms of the common realm we publicly share with each other: "the world." We use the expression "the world" to represent a general framework within which we can locate particular items and their significance. Thus, when faced with the unknown, we may ask: "What in the world is that?" Or when we are perplexed by someone's course of conduct, we may ask: "How in the world could she have done that?"

The world constitutes a general framework for everything with which we are familiar — persons, things, events, ideas. Nor is it just the sum total of these items; it is all these items as they are unified into a totality of relationships to each other. This framework is the setting for efforts to discover "what is true." When we say that something is "true," we imply that we can locate it in a "world" and that we can lead others to its location.

Oftentimes, however, the framework in which we are trying

to locate what is true is neither as fixed nor as unified as the expression "the world" suggests. The limits of our framework may undergo alteration; others may share with us only part of our framework. Thus the denial some may make of what we say is "true" may simply mean that they cannot locate this particular item within a world we share. But there are also circumstances in which this denial will suggest that they and I do not fully share a world: we each may have different frameworks in which to locate persons, events, things, and ideas. Inasmuch as these frameworks overlap, or can be transformed, one into the other, we can each endeavor, with some hope of success, to locate the items that the other calls "true." When these frameworks fail to overlap, however, we shall find ourselves at a loss to deal with one another's claims to truth.

The Moral World: What Ought to Be

The framework that talk of "the world" represents is one on which we ordinarily do not have to focus our attention. The argument that this chapter initiates, however, has to focus upon such a framework because it is an argument by which the possibility will be established that in moral matters — and, most specifically, in regard to freedom — we can determine that which is true. This argument has to establish, therefore, nothing more nor less than the reality of the framework that can be properly called a "moral world." Such a reality is established by showing that there is a common realm that we publicly share with each other, which is constituted in virtue of our interaction with each other, and by reference to which we can ascertain what is morally true about human deeds, dispositions, and events by locating them with reference to this framework.

The idea of a "moral world" has a peculiarity that offers grounds for philosophically argued denials of its reality and of the possibility it offers for determining what is true in moral matters. A moral world is peculiar because it is a world of what ought to be, not of what is. This peculiarity makes problematic any claim to reality for a moral world, inasmuch as reality seems to pertain properly to what is, rather than to what ought to be. It makes equally problematic any determination of truth based on such a framework. Truth seems also to pertain properly to the world of what is, inasmuch as this framework alone seems to stand in common over against each of us; the world of what is, thus, is constituted as the only realm we can publicly share for ascertaining what is true.

Such a philosophically argued denial has an unreflective counterpart in a concern that gives shape to much of today's popular moral thinking and practice. It is a concern to find a sure basis for morality in the results of investigations that tell us what is true in and of the world of what is. If we lose confidence that a particular form of investigation — for example, philosophy — yields results that tell us what is true in and of the world of what is, we cease to look to it for a sure basis on which to form our moral judgments and guide our conduct. We then start to look to other investigations — for example, sociology, psychology — to provide this basis, because we take them to offer us clearer and more concrete access to what is true in and of the world of what is.

This concern for finding a sure basis for morality is well intentioned. It is nonetheless doomed to constant frustration as long as it expects to find that basis, first and foremost, in what is true in and of the world of what is. This expectation is misplaced because it fundamentally misconstrues a basic function of moral thinking and moral practice in our human activity: moral thinking enables us to picture the world and its features as they ought to be, so that our moral practice can change the world, or at least some small part of it, from what it is, to what it ought to be. This function, we should note, rests upon the very peculiarity of the moral world: its portrayal of what ought to be.

In opposition both to this popular concern and its philosophically formulated argumentation, therefore, the argument started in this chapter will show that this peculiarity of a moral world — that it is a world of what ought to be — does not count against its reality. It functions, instead, as a clue to the manner in which we can properly gain access to the reality of this world and to the basis — freedom — that this world provides for truth in moral matters. "Hope" is the most general name we can give to the way we have access to the reality of a world of what ought to be. The particular way in which hope provides such access to reality for our moral thinking and practice will be shown to be the exercise of what we may properly term "moral imagination."[4]

Moral Imagination:
What Ought to Be and the Power to Change the World

Moral imagination designates human efforts to represent a world of what ought to be — that is, the totality of conditions under which moral living is possible. Such efforts are numerous and varied. They range from attempts to picture in detail the social, economic, political, and educational arrangements that are expected to be most conducive to aligning conduct in accord with what is good (e.g., Plato's *Republic*), to efforts to respond to the challenge, prompted in informal moral discussion, of picturing the circumstances or results of "everyone's doing it." Not every exercise of moral imagination requires that we picture explicitly the entire range of conditions that make moral living possible; we can usually presume that many features of the world represented in moral imagination — the world of what ought to be — are quite the same as the world we implicitly represent for all the other purposes of our daily living — the world of what is.

This presumption underscores the particular function of the power possessed by a representation of what ought to be: to move us to change the world of what is, to make it accord better with the representation of a world of what ought to be. Thus, the world of what is, in which I make and attempt to keep promises, has many features, not the least of which are my own interests and inclinations, which work to impede both the making and the keeping of promises. Yet it has other features that work to foster the making and the keeping of promises. If, in our own promise-making, we keep in view just the world of what is, in its ambiguous state both of fostering and impeding promises, we shall generate for each other little confidence in our mutual ability to keep promises. Our confidence in the ability we each have to keep promises can be made more secure insofar as we keep in view what ought to be: the shape that the world will take in virtue of our keeping promises. The world of what is will not take such a shape unless we keep our promises; yet the keeping of a particular promise cannot wait upon the world's fully taking this shape. Thus, in keeping a particular promise we are moved by what ought to be, even though it is not fully actual. The actions we take to keep that promise give to the world of what is a shape that puts it more in accord with what ought to be. These actions thus bring closer to full actuality the world of what ought to be, even though their ground is that world even prior to its actuality.

As an illustration of this power that representations of the world of what ought to be have to move us to action, consider the dramatic situation Kant portrays in the *Critique of Practical Reason:* the man threatened by his sovereign with sudden death unless he perjures himself against an innocent man whom the ruler seeks to destroy.[5] Kant claims that we have no hesitation in judging what the morally proper course of conduct has to be: to refuse to swear falsely. His claim has intuitive plausibility, even though it is clear that the ground for surety in this case cannot be from the world of what is. In that world, more often than not, tyrants carry out their threats, and for everyone who refuses to swear falsely under threats, there is likely to be someone else more compliant. The world of what is could give us surety only that the outcome will be the working of evil. Yet, in the face of that truth and the surety it gives, there is, as Kant presents the case, an even greater surety that the morally appropriate course of conduct is to refuse to swear falsely, come what may. That surety can be understood as confidence in a principle that is true of the world that ought to be: the life and the person of a human individual is never to be put at the disposal of anyone's whim, ambition, or desire. Peculiar to this truth, and others like it, is that it displays how things must be, even though they clearly are not yet that way in the world of what is. Peculiar to it also is the power it has to shape our judgment and conduct precisely in virtue of what ought to be, despite the failure of the way things now are to stand in accord with the representation of what ought to be.

The power that representations of what ought to be have to move us to action suggests a way to understand how a moral world can be quite real. Its reality is a function of its power to move us to change the world of what is. The argument I am initiating will show that this power has its basis in our human capacity to fashion a shared world. My argument will show that this capacity, as it gives shape to human conduct, is freedom. It is a freedom, however, that has been directed to what is real and true through the exercise of moral imagination, which functions to represent what ought to be as a world that can be shared by each and by all. In effect, this argument will show that what ought to be is real and true in virtue of the power it has to call upon that which makes us fully human: our mutuality, the capacity to share freely of ourselves. Moral imagination plays a central role in this argument because through it we are enabled to envision the full range of this capacity to share freely of ourselves, and to shape our dispositions and actions in accord with this capacity.

To move this argument, from its initial consideration of "the world," along a direction that will lead us to the mutuality central to freedom, we have to turn to the forms of moral imagination that represent a world of what ought to be in a way that shows it to be fully shareable by each and by all. One of these forms is moral theory; another is the literary form of the extended narrative. Despite their apparently radical differences, narrative and moral theory each has power to move us to act to change the world of what is to accord better with the world of what ought to be. They have this power insofar as they invite us to become a part of the world they represent no matter how much some of its particular features differ from the world of what is.

Moral Imagination as Moral Theory

Let us first consider how moral theory presents us with a world in which we can share and which can move us to act to change the world of what is. The typology of moral agency developed by H. Richard Niebuhr in *The Responsible Self* offers an analysis that instances these points. Teleological and deontological moral theories offer different images of human agency, which they invite us to share both as tools for understanding and as guides for action. The abstract rendering each theory gives to the ordered totality of relationships among persons and what they do takes basic shape from a particular image of moral agency that is deemed primary. The activities of the artisan and of the citizen provide models of moral agency, respectively, for teleological and for deontological accounts of human moral phenomena. The moral world that is ordered in accord with the image of artisan is different from the moral world ordered in accord with the image of citizen. In the former, the attainment of good as our own achievement shapes moral endeavor, and action is measured by the good that is its outcome. In the latter, the will to discover and do what is right shapes moral endeavor, and action is measured by the rectitude with which it is undertaken and faithfully completed.[6]

These different images of human moral existence — and those of artisan and citizen are not the only ones we employ — not only give shape to the theories we fashion to account for human moral phenomena; they also give direction to our efforts to govern conduct in accord with such theories. In the moral world of the human maker, we will bend our efforts to the maximizing of good. Our most perplexing moral dilemmas will arise when it seems that no good can arise, no matter what we do or fail to do, or when we must determine which good to effect and for whom. In the moral world of the human citizen, we will bend our efforts to cultivating the dispositions and establishing the institutions conducive to a willing observance of the rules of right and fair conduct. Our most perplexing moral dilemmas will arise when it seems that observance of one rule puts us in conflict with observance of another of equally compelling force or when the observance of a rule formulated to effect fairness effects, to our chagrin, injustice instead. In the world of the human maker, the most valued moral skill will be clarity in one's perception of what is good. In the world of the human citizen, it will be steadfastness in the observance of the rules of right and fair conduct.

On Niebuhr's analysis, these two types of theories have dominated Western moral thinking and practice inasmuch as their underlying images capture experiences already shared by most members of Western culture; they then call us to extend that experience by making the image an interpretive guide to the full range of our conduct.[7] In so doing, we make the image the model by which to shape, through our conduct, a world that ought to be. Niebuhr then offers a third image — the "responsible self," the person in dialogue with others and the world — as a basis for his own moral theory. His development of this image offers a more complete instance of how moral imagination functions in moral theory: this image, more so than that of maker or of citizen, calls us to take part in a world that is not yet but ought to be, so that we may be moved to change the world of what is. In Niebuhr's theory, the world of what ought to be is dialogical; the world of what is as yet is only partly dialogical. The image of the responsible self calls upon us to engage each other in a dialogue of thought, word, action, and disposition, in order to bring into dialogue that which is not yet fully so, and which would remain as it is unless we engage it.[8]

Moral Imagination as Narrative

Niebuhr's typology offers a straightforward way of exhibiting the function of moral imagination in moral theory. There is no corresponding way, unfortunately, by which I can straightforwardly exhibit the way narrative functions as moral imagination. This function is not simply equivalent to the use to which narrative may be put to illuminate or to enrich moral theory. That use builds upon the imaginative character of narrative to represent in a concrete, explicit, and sustained fashion a world that is no longer, or has not been, or is yet to be. Narrative thereby provides a context, larger than the world of what is, against which particular images underlying moral theory can be elaborated. Their adequacy to serve as representations of human moral existence can be thus ascertained more thoroughly. The worlds of citizenship, in which, for instance, Socrates in the *Crito*, and Captain Vere, in *Billy Budd*, live, decide, and act, show us the complexity of the image of citizen, as well as the limitations of its claim to be adequate for representing the full range of human moral existence.

This use of narrative to provide a context for the elaboration of images of human moral existence does not, however, constitute the only, or the most basic, way it functions as moral imagination. If this were the only way for it so to function, then the cautionary tale would be the ideal form for putting narrative to a moral use: "The moral of the story is. . . ." Use of narrative only in this way renders moral imagination even more parochial than any moral theory it attempts to illustrate and inculcate through such tales.

The more fundamental way in which narrative functions as moral imagination rests on its power to bring us to identify with others. This identification takes place on a number of levels. Narrative calls on us to recognize how like we are to those about whom the tale is told. It makes it possible for us to become aware how like we are to all who with us listen to the tale. It even suggests that we are each capable of telling the tale to those who have not yet heard it. In retelling the tale to them, we widen the circle of those we find like us. Narrative thereby functions to place us in contexts that manifest our human communality in ways so basic that merely the simple telling and listening acknowledge them. Narrative, by its very form, invites us to exhibit humanity in a very full way: in telling, listening, and retelling, we find that we are sharing freely of ourselves.

Narrative: Human Communality as the Frame of the Moral World

By manifesting human communality to us, narrative makes concretely present to us one element that is basic for constituting the framework that I have designated as a "moral world." As human communality is made manifest in particular narratives, however, it is not all of one kind. In fact, the very multiplicity and multiformity of the ways it can be told that we are like one another results in narrative seemingly presenting to us not a single "moral world," but a bewildering array of "worlds," many of which we would be reluctant to term, in any ordinary sense, "moral." Instead of a common realm that we can publicly share, each individual narrative often seems to offer us a partial glimpse of a world that is the singular vision of the teller of the particular tale.

This irreducible particularity of the individual narrative seems to preclude taking any one human communality that a single narrative manifests as more basic than any other. This, consequently, seems also to preclude appeal to a specific, concrete communality as a basis for constituting a common realm to function as a moral world. It even suggests that the very idea of a moral "world" is incoherent: our varied ways of being like each other cannot be unified into a common realm that functions to locate human deeds, dispositions, and events in their moral significance.

The particularity of individual narratives, and the multiplicity of the human communalities they manifest to us, however, does not require that we despair of finding a specific human communality adequate to constitute a moral world; nor does it require that we give up as incoherent the idea of a moral world. This is so because a very condition for the particularity of individual narratives and the multiplicity of human communalities that they represent is that common realm already constituted and specified as a fundamental condition for our interaction with each other. In virtue of the common realm this condition provides, we can, and do, albeit often in a limited fashion, identify ourselves as like one another: before we are able to articulate the particular ways of likeness, we already acknowledge our likeness through interacting with one another. This first acknowledgment of human action is the simplest and most unqualified: "I am like her: she is like me." Without this first and most basic acknowledgment, there would be no point to the telling of particular likenesses.

Narrative first presupposes the identification we make with one another in virtue of our interaction. Narrative then makes this identification concrete, but not just for the moments in which the narrative is told. It is rather the case that the most important way in which narrative makes this identification concrete for us concerns the past and the future. Narrative enables past and future to function concretely as a fundamental context for our continuity both as individuals and as humans. It takes the moment of recognition — "I am like her; she is like me" — and allows us to extend it in time — "We have been like each other; we will remain like each other." This continuity is an especially important element for constituting a moral world. It functions to locate in a "world" — that is, in a place for truth — the moral significance of the deeds of our lives as they intersect with the deeds and lives of others.

Narrative provides us with a hold upon the continuity of our lives, and the significance of that continuity for the truth of moral matters, by making it possible for the past, as history, and the future, as hope, to function in the constitution of a moral world.[9] They each function as a way for publicly sharing the common realm that is constituted by our interaction with each other. The full establishment of this point is particularly important for the foundation that I hope my argument will provide for the enterprise of moral theology. This is so because a world in which history and hope function as ways for the public sharing of a common realm is the one in which the quest of faith for understanding must take place, if it is to present itself as an intelligible human enterprise. The full establishment of this point, however, must wait upon the resolution of more basic matters about the way a moral world is constituted to provide us with access to what is true. All that has been indicated so far is that the frame of a moral world is our likeness to one another, and that moral imagination provides at least two ways — moral theory and narrative — for us to represent such likeness in concrete form, so that we can locate the moral significance of our deeds and dispositions, and the events that shape our lives.

Human Communality: Tales of our Going on Together

The two points just mentioned are necessary preliminaries to the steps of my argument that will show more directly the connections between moral imagination and truth. These steps will also make it possible to specify in greater detail how likeness to one another serves as the frame of a moral world. It so serves in virtue of the power of moral imagination: we can envision our likeness to one another in forms that allow us to exercise to the full our capacity to share freely of ourselves. These forms of likeness to one another are ones we most often find only fitfully and partially in the world of what is. They are the forms of likeness to one another that allow us to place trust in each other, to pledge care for one another, to rely upon each other's word, and to live faithfully to the pledges of trust we have made with each other. These forms of likeness are, in one sense, "ideal"; yet, in virtue of the powers they offer us to change the world of what is, they constitute what is most fundamentally true and real in a moral world. Narrative has a particularly important role to play in our comprehension of the "ideality" of the forms of likeness that constitute the frame of a moral world. The forms of likeness that imagination enables us to envision cannot be such as to render our particularities powerless for the service of human mutuality; they become such when our comprehension of them becomes abstract — that is, separated from the narratives that tell concretely of their recognition.

We can see results of this kind, I believe, in some of the problems our society has had, particularly in the last three decades, in dealing with issues of race and ethnicity. "Separate but equal" was finally seen as morally flawed at its very base by its effectively precluding the possibility of black and white going on together in American society. Yet, since that judgment was rendered into public doctrine, black and white have struggled with, at best, partial success, to find or fashion a communality, a likeness to one another, that can serve as an effective, positive, and shared basis for going on together. Events of the past three decades have all too often unmasked ideals of "integration," "participation," and the like, as far too abstract to deal with the kinds of particularity that concretely obstruct human goings on together — for example, economic power, social position, fear, anger, despair. Ironically, just as the inability of these ideals to support effectively a going on together needful for our society was being disclosed, awareness of, and pride in, the particularities of race and ethnicity increased. In the absence of an effective positive ideal for going on together, these particularities lend themselves all too readily to effect a result that is the polar opposite of the hope to which acknowledgment of our likeness gives rise; they effect, not a going on together, but a setting apart from one another.

One could, perhaps too simply but not wholly inaccurately, describe this situation as the loss of confidence in the story of the "melting pot." What truth that tale had was effective for placing at least some particularities in service of our interdependence — though at the cost, no doubt, of denying other particularities, such as one's native language, of at least equal importance. As long as credit could be placed in that story, moreover, we did not find the likenesses presupposed in ideals such as "integration" or "participation" to be abstract; they could function effectively in providing guidance for the public realm of our dealings with one another.

We need not spend undue time mourning the loss of the "melting pot" story. Of more pressing concern is the fact that we seem to have no tale to tell in its place.

The same absence of tales of going on together to which we can all give credence seems, more recently, to have affected our dealings with one another as male and female. Here most especially we seem to be in need both of acknowledging the likenesses that enable identification and trust, and of acknowledging the particularities that enable us to be both different and interdependent.[10] Here it seems that soon, without tales effective of such acknowledgments, particularities will again find themselves put to use — as they inevitably are when we can see ourselves only as strangers to one another — for division, isolation, and, finally, domination.

Human Communality and the Truth of Morality

In the world of what is, it is not always easy to see or to acknowledge the likenesses that enable us to identify with and to trust one another. Often it is far more difficult to see our particularities and differences as suited, and even called, to the fostering of interdependence. The next part of my argument, therefore, will make a point that is fundamental for establishing the way in which we can ascertain what is true in moral matters: the basic forms of our likeness to one another that allow us to exercise, in and through our particularities and differences, our capacity to share freely of ourselves, cannot be found by considering them as elements just of the world of what is. They are rather forms of human communality that the world of what ought to be holds out to us as pledge and promise. As a result, we can establish that what we speak of as "true" in moral matters takes a form that is proper to a world of what ought to be; that form is pledge and promise.

What is "true," therefore, with regard to the moral character of human deeds, dispositions, and events, will be measured in terms of their accord with the forms of human communality pledged and promised by a world of what ought to be. It is, moreover, not accidental that, from Plato to Rawls, Western moral thinkers have employed images of republic and city, commonwealth and kingdom, to set the context for their moral theories. These images represent the fact that the forms of human communality, pledged and promised by a world of what ought to be, have an essentially public character.

This public character of the human communalities that are to serve as the measure of truth for moral matters has important consequences for the way moral imagination, in each of its guises, functions as the way to such truth. Some of these consequences, the most important of which concern the representation of human good, will be noted at appropriate places in the elaboration, in the following section, of the steps of my argument that show that truth takes the form of pledge and promise in a world of what ought to be. These consequences will then be considered in greater detail in the discussions of human destiny found in chapters 3 and 4.

II. THE TRUTH OF MORALITY:
PLEDGE AND PROMISE

What Ought to Be: Pledge of the Moral Future

A world of what ought to be has the power to shape our judgments and to move us to action. The example from Kant cited in the previous section is plausible in virtue of this power. The same power is instanced, usually in a less dramatic fashion, each time we act in accord with the principle that the life and person of a human individual is not to be put at the disposal of anyone's whim, ambition, or desire. In the world of what is, and according to what is true of it, we find ourselves all too often putting others at the disposal of our whims, ambitions, and desires, and in turn being put at their disposal in the same way. In accord with a principle of a world that ought to be, however, we have granted to us the power both to judge that such treatment of persons is not to be, and to act so that such treatment does not come to be. Particular judgments and actions in accord with this principle instance it in its form as pledge and promise. Bringing such treatment to a stop now, in a single instance, cannot by itself convey the full power of the principle that the life and person of a human individual is never to be put at the disposal of anyone's whim, ambition, or desire. Such particular judgments and actions cannot anticipate, save in a rare paradigmatic instance, the multifarious forms that efforts to place others at our disposal take. To convey the full import of the principle, the judgment that this is not to be now must, therefore, also stand as a pledge that neither will it be hereafter; so, too, the action taken in accord with that judgment.

This point can be put in more general form: moral principles exhibit what is true of a world of what ought to be in the form of a pledge and promise of the moral future. The enterprise of morality requires that we be ready to place greater confidence in the truth of the future as it is represented in moral principles than we do in the truth of the present or of the past — neither of which can claim to instance fully what ought to be. Kant's example provides a case in point: the person who abides by the judgment and decision to refuse to swear falsely has greater confidence in the truth of a moral ordering of a world that does not yet exist, but which is just, than in the truth of the world of what is, but which shows that person the strength of the sovereign's motivation and the perils facing one's own resoluteness.

Confidence in the truth of a moral ordering of the world empowers the resolution to abide by the judgment and decision not to swear falsely even though such ordering has not been fully or clearly instanced in the world of what is. This does not mean that the world of what is shows no moral ordering; rather, the moral ordering it shows is not sufficient of itself to shape our judgments or to move us to action in ways that exercise to the full our capacity to share fully of ourselves. Such sufficiency will be supplied in virtue of the exercise of moral imagination. In particular, it will be supplied insofar as moral imagination represents for us the most fundamental pledge and promise of the moral future that a world of what ought to be offers to us: the possibility of human community in its fulness.

Human Likeness: Pledge of Human Community

What starts as the acknowledgment of likeness — the simplest and most basic moment of human communality — ends in the fulness of human community. This, in effect, sums up the route on which moral imagination places us, and the destination to which it offers us guidance. Moral imagination places us on this route by making it possible for us to catch sight of our human likenesses, and to see even the most pronounced of our particularities as capacities for interdependence. Our interaction with one another constitutes our entrance into a moral world and, in consequence, carries an implicit acknowledgment of human likeness. This implicit acknowledgment is yet not adequate for determining what is true in moral matters, inasmuch as the specific purposes of interaction are met by a partial acknowledgment when it is made explicit: "I am like you in this way, just for these purposes." The human likeness that constitutes the frame of a moral world is, by contrast, simple and unqualified in its affirmation: "I am like her; she is like me." Though simple and unqualified, it is not thereby indeterminate; as we shall see in the next chapter it is the concrete likeness constituted by freedom as the very condition for our interaction. It is therefore left to moral imagination to make us aware in a reflective manner of our entrance into the moral world as it is constituted by our simple and unqualified likeness to each other, presupposed as the very condition for interaction with each other. Moral imagination brings us to the recognition that one who, in so many particulars, is, and can be, not like to me, is, for all that, still like to me and I, like to her.

If it is correct to locate our entrance into a moral world in the acknowledgment of likeness, this suggests the kind of narrative that brings us to and then across the threshold: the tales that recount the meeting with and the treatment of the stranger.[11] To welcome the stranger is to act in accord with the hope that gives human moral life its power: it is the hope that, even with one so different, there can be a going on together. In many tales, that hope takes its concrete form as hospitality. The shared meal and roof may be the only going on together one may have with this stranger; but for others who may come after — as well as for this stranger, with the next who welcome her — the going on together this sharing pledges may have a more enduring completion.

We should not forget that these tales have their dark side, which is a consequence of failing to act on the hope of going on together. There is the stranger not welcomed, whom the tales that cut to the very core reveal as more like us than we dared imagine or dread. There is the person we should know as most like us whom we cast aside as even less than a stranger: thus we have the tales of Oedipus, of Joseph and his brothers, and many more.

Whether concretely in narrative, or more abstractly in moral theory, moral imagination sets us at a complex task by making us reflectively aware of our entrance into a moral world. The simple and most basic moment of human communality — the fundamental acknowledgment of our human likeness — does not remain simple for long in the face of the particular exigencies of human thought and action. A simple affirmation of human likeness appears far too sweeping to serve as a guide for shaping ac-

tions undertaken for quite particular human purposes. The task
to which we are thereby set is one of giving specific determina-
tions to our human likeness, which nonetheless hold us to the
simple and unqualified affirmation of likeness that constituted
our reflective entry into a moral world. Moral imagination serves
as an instrument for this task in both of its guises: narrative and
moral theory.

In each of these guises moral imagination serves multiple functions. As moral theory, for instance, it enables us to keep in view
a simple and unqualified affirmation of human likeness as the
frame of a moral world. This is accomplished on the basis of the
concepts that a moral theory employs to represent what it takes
to be our most basic human communality. Communalities of "nature," of "sympathetic feeling," of "striving" and "will" are among
the ones that moral theory has frequently employed to denote
what is acknowledged by our reflective entrance into a moral
world. In the guise of narrative, moral imagination also keeps
us in mind of the fundamental acknowledgment of human likeness. Narrative provides, in its concrete tales, opportunities to
glimpse yet again, now from a different perspective, now in virtue of a different particularity, that we have been, are, and shall
continue to be like each other and to depend upon one another.

Moral theory and narrative also function to help us specify
the more determinate forms of human likeness that correspond
to the particular exigencies of our action. Rarely, if ever, is my
action called out from my communality as human in its simple
and unqualified form; it is called out from me as worker, as citizen, as brother or sister, as friend, as colleague, and the like.
Moral theory and narrative provide ways for me to recognize
and to denote these more particular human communalities out
of which my action is being called.

Finally, moral theory and narrative both function to place the
more determinate forms of our human likeness in proper relationship to the simple and unqualified acknowledgment of likeness that is the frame of a moral world. This function is the one
that is most important for establishing that pledge and promise
are the form for what is true in and of a moral world. This is
so because moral imagination — particularly, though not exclusively, in the guise of narrative — enables us to place the more
determinate forms of our human likeness into a relationship with

the simple and unqualified acknowledgment of our human likeness that holds out to us the possibility of human community in its fulness.[12]

This last point can be formulated more simply and more boldly. Through moral imagination a world of what ought to be holds this fundamental promise out to us: there is to be full achievement of human community. If what is true of a moral world takes the form of pledge and promise, then we may say that this promise of the full achievement of human community is the fundamental truth of morality.

Narrative and the Promise of Human Destiny

The claim of this promise to be a form of truth, and to be itself true, cannot be separated from the vehicle of the promise: moral imagination. This promise makes its claim to truth through moral imagination in two ways: in moral theory, as an account of what constitutes the most fundamental human good, and in narrative, as the representation of that good in concrete form. The claim it makes through moral theory will be examined in detail in chapter 3; the claim it makes through narrative will be discussed both here and in chapter 4. This twofold treatment is required because there is a complex relationship between narrative and moral theory in their representations of human good. Narrative enables us to represent concretely the human good that sets us on the path of going on together; moral theory, in turn, then enables us to represent that good in terms large enough to encompass all the particularities of our going on together. Moral theory, though it allows us to represent the possibility that our going on together will endure into the fulness of human community — a possibility promised in narrative's first setting us on this path — cannot provide us with full assurance that this possibility will be realized. The task of providing such assurance falls on narrative. It fulfills that task by representing to us, in its particularity, the good that is the end and completion of the path of human mutuality and interdependence on which it set us and for which moral theory has served as guide.

Although the specific argument presented in this volume requires an account of the relationship between moral theory and narrative in their representations of human good, such an account also serves a larger purpose: it helps mark off some of the more important aspects of what has been termed the congruence, compatibility, and cooperation of reason with faith, and of philosophy with theology. Hope serves as the focus of the account I give of the relationship between moral theory and narrative in their representation of human good. Hope understood as such a focus is not without significance for the broader questions of the relationship between reason and faith, and between philosophy and theology. Hope is, in many ways, the most appropriate focus for discussing these various relationships; in it can be shown, I believe, many of their central features.

Hope is a curious concept. The philosophical discussion I propose in the next chapter avails itself of Kant's insights that hope stands at the juncture of human knowledge and human action and that the focus of hope must be communal — that is, not just for oneself, but for one another. Ironically, Kant's insights have often been taken seriously by those — most notably, Hegelians and Marxists — who would have us freed from assent to the very limitations of the human finitude that make those insights possible.[13] Far less frequently have they been taken seriously by the enterprise of Christian theology, which takes place in a community whose very existence gives testimony to the acceptance — empowered, it is true, by grace — of human finitude.

The origin of hope in an acknowledgment of human finitude is central for specifying the relationships between reason and faith, and between philosophy and theology. This acknowledgment requires that the hope that we base on the power of reason to understand and to govern conduct itself exhibit our finitude: we hope for much — for the full achievement of human community — but in fact what we hope for is beyond our human power to achieve for ourselves. What faith then shows us is that, even in hoping for much, we have not hoped completely, for what is to be given to us is a share in the very life of God. What reason enables us to hope for is not what God promises and gives — because that far exceeds our hopes. Reason is not eschatological vision, yet what it allows us to hope for is given, too, in consequence of God's promise and gift.

This acknowledgment of human finitude also serves to delimit the roles moral theory and narrative play in representing human good. Narrative stands at the beginning: it is whatever tale we tell of the acknowledging of human likeness that engaged us in our own particularity. This is the tale in which I acknowledge the central moral feature of human finitude: that I do not stand at the center of the universe; that there is someone else — whether it first be parent, teacher, brother, sister, friend, or even stranger — whom I have come to acknowledge, who, by being who he or she is, without denying my particularity, now stands as focus for my understanding and action.[14]

Hope and the Focus of our World

This is an acknowledgment difficult both to live and to tell — particularly in a culture such as ours, which undercuts our capacity to imagine and to assent to the truth of such a shift, away from ourselves, in the focus of our understanding and action. To younger college students it is often an acknowledgment of which they can make little sense: often they have not been pulled out of their own world of immediacy through the study of literature or history. They all too often see and live their relationships with parents and family as the opposition of dependence to independence — a view that, ironically, parents are not always reluctant themselves to adopt — rather than as an opportunity to learn the skills of interdependence. Similarly, they all too often see and attempt to live their relationships with one another in terms of our culture's measures of self-worth, few of which serve to develop the skills for going on together, or to suggest that there can be more to going on together than moments of shared immediacy.

This acknowledgment, without which it makes no sense to speak of human good, must touch us in our particularity. For the students I have described, as for us all, the ways we can be touched in our particularity to occasion this acknowledgment are multiform: a friend's loyalty — or a call upon our loyalty; the trauma of the death of a parent or of a friend; learning the skills of a love that is more than the acting out of adolescent anxieties; these are just a few. It is not enough, however, simply to be touched in our particularity. We must be able to make sense of being so touched. We make sense of it most directly as narrative — by telling of our being so touched and by locating it in the course of our lives. Our own skill for telling this tale of ourselves, moreover, rests in large measure upon our having heard told the tales of others who have been so touched. One reason why it seems especially difficult for young college students — though certainly not them alone — to formulate and to make sense of the tale being told in their own lives that shows them not to stand at the center of the universe is that we have all almost ceased to tell — or to listen attentively to — the literature, the poetry, the drama, the history that tells that tale and alerts us to its telling in our own lives.[15]

Narrative stands at the beginning of our representation of human good, enabling us to acknowledge its basis in our likeness to one another and our need for one another. Once we are set on the path of going on together that it shows us, moral theory then functions to guide our conduct in accord with its own way of representing human good. In contrast to narrative, which draws our attention to good in and through its particularity, moral theory requires that we focus our attention upon those dimensions of good that, though found in particularity, have larger, and even universal import.

Hope and the Endurance of Mutuality

Moral theory enables us to represent the acknowledgment of our likeness and interdependence in a simple and unconditioned form, and to make that acknowledgment a standard for our conduct. It also enables us to represent, as the hope that our going on together will endure, the mutuality to which our conduct's exercise of freedom is ordered. This, too, can function to shape our conduct. In consequence, we employ moral theory to remind us that our conduct is required to seek good in each and every particularity of our going on together.

For moral theory to function in this way, one need not have mastered, in the manner of a trained philosopher, its conceptual intricacies. Moral theory functions this way in the reflectively ordered conduct of the person of enduring good conscience. For that person, there is frequently no need to refer explicitly to moral theory's proper ways of representing human good for purposes of guiding our conduct.[16] The need and importance of its ways of representing good becomes apparent, however, when we consider those circumstances in which efforts are made to render impotent the power to do good, by systematically removing the conditions that allow one to be touched by good in its particularity.

Solzhenitsyn's descriptions of the Gulag provide a paradigm for such circumstances: a world of mistrust, in which the standard of likeness was the degradation of each in his or her own particularity, and in which hope for even the minimum of human mutuality was extinguished. Yet even in these circumstances there were those who held on to an acknowledgment of human likeness in the simple and unconditioned form that guides human conduct to good; they sustained that acknowledgment and acted in accord with it in full awareness, moreover, that, in the world of the Gulag, it would not be allowed to have the least efficacy for establishing or for sustaining conditions for even minimal human mutuality.[17]

There are two points to note here. The first bears upon moral theory's representing of human good; more specifically, it bears upon moral theory's representing of the acknowledgment of our human likeness and interdependence to be of unconditional and of universal import. In representing this acknowledgment this way, moral theory affirms that we are each required to sustain that acknowledgment, even if we find ourselves cut off from the particularities from which it issued and which ordinarily sustain it: once we have acknowledged our human communality and its requirements for our conduct, it is at peril to our moral existence that we later deny it, whatever be our reasons. Those who, in Solzhenitsyn's account of the Gulag, sustained, in the integrity of their vision and conduct, an acknowledgment of human likeness in its simple and unconditioned form, confirmed the legitimacy of moral theory's requirement and the truth of its proper way of representing human good.

The second point bears on narrative's representing of human good. Although what was sustained by those few giants of Solzhenitsyn's account can be understood in terms of moral theory's manner of representing good, that which enabled them to sustain such an acknowledgment of human likeness cannot similarly be understood fully by reference to moral theory. It is not without significance that, of the few who sustained an acknowledgment of human likeness in the simple and unqualified form that guides human conduct to good, many did so in virtue of a hope whose focus was not on effecting mutuality in this age but upon the God who transcends this and every human age.[18]

The acknowledgment of likeness was sustained not on the basis of moral theory, but on hope. It is by no means implausible to characterize this sustaining hope in terms of narrative: those who sustained an acknowledgment of human likeness enabling for good, even in the all-encompassing desperation of the Gulag, did so because they could see even those particularities as part of a tale, now dimly and fitfully understood, in which that likeness is not and never can be lost. It cannot be lost, because promises have been made for its abiding preservation.

This suggests a further and final role for narrative, in which it brings to completion its initial representation of human good. Narrative now stands at the end of our path of going on together as the tale in which a promise is made and kept that this path, on which we were set by the acknowledgment of our likeness and interdependence, has an end and completion. Just as in the beginning, moreover, the role of narrative here is focused on particularity. There is, however, a difference: the particularity on which this tale invites us to focus is God's particularity — his particularity in making Jesus Christ the concrete term and effective sign of the good we have been enabled to hope to attain in full measure.[19]

In order for us to see the very need for this representation of human good and the appropriateness of narrative's providing it, we must be able to make sense of a hope that, though it originates in an acknowledgment of human good in all its diversity, variety, and complexity, focuses its completion into and upon the particularity of Jesus Christ. Making full sense of this hope would resolve, as well, issues that are central to determining the appropriate relationships between reason and faith and between philosophy and theology. I do not propose what I offer here, and in the rest of my argument, to be such a making of full sense of this hope: I offer it only as a start. Just as at the beginning of our path of going on together we must be touched in our particularity in order to acknowledge our likeness and our dependence upon one another, so, too, to catch sight of the end of the path we must be touched in our particularity. Being so touched involves what Christian theology calls "faith": we are touched in our particularity by the particularity of God's love in Jesus Christ.

This latter touching is not entirely discontinuous, however, with our first setting on the path, nor with our efforts, guided by moral theory, to stay on it. To the extent that each of these gives us hope for the completion of human mutuality — that our going on together will endure — they place us in readiness for being so touched that we might see the path's end. They may not, it is true, fully prepare us to see that the path's end will be found in the particularity of Jesus Christ; that is, and remains, the "scandal" of the historical character of Christian faith.[20] They cannot, however, preclude the possibility of our being so touched: for if they do, the hope they offer us — that our going will endure — will prove, in the end, to be ill founded.

The good that narrative, in its latter role, represents and, as will be shown later, helps bring to be, is that for which moral theory's most adequate representation is the satisfaction of human cravings in virtue of the full achievement of human community. Narrative shows this to be far more than is presented us in moral theory's representation; that satisfaction is shown to be in nothing other than the very life of God, shared with us as gift. The fundamental basis for narrative's power to show us this has been put in bold form by the novelist and essayist Reynolds Price:

> The root of story sprang from need — need for companionship and consolation by a creature as vulnerable, four million years ago and now, as any protozoan in a warm brown swamp. The need is not for the total consolation of narcotic fantasy — our own will performed in airless triumph — but for credible news that our lives proceed in order toward a pattern which, if tragic here and now, is ultimately pleasing in the mind of a god who sees a totality and *at last* enacts His will. We crave nothing less than the perfect story; and while we chatter or listen all our lives in a din of craving — jokes, anecdotes, novels, dreams, films, plays, songs, half the words of our days — we are satisfied only by the one short tale we feel to be true: *History is the will of a just god who knows us.*[21]

The claim Price makes for narrative is simple and daring: all the tales we tell, however varied they may be, are over and over

saying to us: "History is the will of a just god who knows us."
This claim provides narrative with the power to bring to completion the task to which it initially set our moral existence: the
recognition of human likeness. It completes that initial role by
locating even more fundamentally the likeness that narrative first
enabled us to recognize: that likeness is in the destiny to which
we have been called, to share in God's own life.

In this section I have sought to establish that truth takes the
form of pledge and promise in a world of what ought to be. I
have indicated that this claim serves as part of a larger argument to establish the reality of the framework that I have termed
a "moral world." The argument for the claim that truth takes
the form of pledge and promise in a world of what ought to be
has taken the form of an explication of the function of moral
imagination in representing our human likenesses to each other.
Price's claim about narrative now makes it possible to show why
the argument has proceeded this way. His claim indicates what
is most at stake in the recognition of our human liknesses: the
possibility of a human destiny, not altogether of our own making, in which we are each to share in full.

From the perspective provided by Price's claim we can see the
argument proceeding thus: we can acknowledge that we are fundamentally like each other; the likeness we acknowledge holds
out the possibility of becoming a basis on which we can learn
to live with each other. We represent this possibility as a hope,
or at least a desire, for the achievement of human community.
The likeness we recognize thereby functions as a promise of human community. Representing it as a basis upon which we can
fashion human community can be considered a fundamental exercise of moral imagination.

This exercise of imagination, however, must take form as hope,
because the concrete forms of our human likeness often offer quite
meager grounds upon which to form human community. Thus
the promise of human community is a bold one, but it can be
a far-from-convincing one. It will be an empty promise, moreover, if its keeping is simply left up to us: though we can boldly
envision the possibility of the full achievement of human community, the community we actually achieve is so fragile and transitory that, even at its best, it is but an obscure reflection of what
either moral theory or narrative enables us to envision as full

achievement. If, however, we can be sure of a narrative that tells us that history is the will of a just God who knows us, then there is a basis on which we can rely for the keeping of the promise of human community. This basis is a power that is "beyond" us, but that is as it must be, given that the promise that has been made is beyond our power to fulfill. Both the promise and the power by which the promise is kept are given to us in a primary manner through narrative. Because they are given through narrative, imagination is thereby constituted as a fundamental human mode for attaining truth.

The initial exposition of the argument that truth takes the form of pledge and promise in a world of what ought to be was thus offered on the basis of the representation of human likeness by moral imagination. The fundamental pledge made on the basis of the human likeness represented in moral imagination was taken to bear upon the full achievement of human community; such achievement is what a moral world most fundamentally promises us. Price's remarks about narrative, however, suggest something more fundamental about the representation of human likeness when moral imagination is at work in that guise. The power of narrative to engage the basic cravings of teller and listener for an enduring going on together manifests that our human likeness to one another is one whose fundamental significance rests upon the destiny offered us by a transcendent God. The manifestation in narrative of this likeness has an important consequence for the full achievement of moral community pledged by a world of what ought to be. The consequence is simple but wide-reaching: this likeness gives an unshakable assurance that the pledge will be redeemed, the promise kept. It is an assurance that our human destiny will take its form in accord with our capacity to share freely of ourselves.

In the light of the possibilities that Price's remarks have suggested, the argument that truth takes the form of pledge and promise in a world of what ought to be has consequences that are particularly useful for the enterprise of elaborating a philosophical foundation for moral theology. The most important is that it will allow us to represent more exactly human community in accord with that character of mutuality most fundamentally pledged and promised by a world of what ought to be. We can envision the full achievement of mutuality in a world of what ought to be as the fundamental condition needed for satisfying, for each and for all, our basic cravings.

This consequence is not an obvious one. In fact, as I have already suggested and will elaborate in detail in the next section, the human likenesses from which we draw the pledge of the full achievement of human community do not seem adequate as a basis to govern our conduct for the full achievement of human community. Thus the full achievement of human community, upon which the satisfaction of our cravings depends, is not within our power to effect. What is pledged and promised, therefore, seems doubly unattainable, and, thus, contrary to what I have been arguing, a most unlikely candidate to be considered "true."

Grounds for the eventual resolution of this difficulty will be found in the next section, in a consideration of the function of "hope" in the transformation of even such partial and particularistic representations of human likeness into representations adequate to the full achievement of human community. I will argue that this transformation is empowered by a human communality that hope draws from narrative. This communality is the finitude of human conduct, which narrative both exhibits and transcends by making the deeds that are told a binding force for human mutuality. I will argue later that the transformation empowered by this communality enables us to direct, through our conduct, the potentiality of our cravings for fostering particular human communalities into practices conducive to the full achievement of human community. As a result, we shall be able to specify, by the end of my argument, in chapter 4, the character of the human community, pledged by a world of what ought to be, which is called for as fundamental condition for the satisfaction of human cravings. This community is, first and foremost, a community of mutuality: a community of those who conscientiously foster the skills that enable the essential interdependence of their lives to work for the attainment of good for one another. Mutuality fostered in this way constitutes the core of the charity or love that in the Catholic tradition has been claimed to be the fundamental form of the life of virtue.[22] Thus the human community that provides a condition fundamental for satisfying, for each and all, our basic human cravings is a community in which charity gives form to virtue.

III. THE DISCIPLINE OF MORAL IMAGINATION: HOPE, MORAL COMMUNITY, AND THE COMPLETION OF DESIRE

Hope and Imagination: From Human Likeness to Human Community

In the course of discussion so far, I have mentioned hope in connection with moral imagination. My argument has now reached a stage at which it becomes useful to explicate this connection in greater detail. At the very outset of my argument, hope was called "the most general name we can give to the way we have access to the reality of a world of what ought to be." Moral imagination was called "the particular way hope provides such access for our moral thinking and practice." Discussion of moral imagination has focused upon its function of representing human likeness, as our point of entry into a moral world; and human community, as the fundamental pledge we can envision such a world to make.

My explication of the connection between hope and moral imagination will begin by noting a feature of the claims already made on behalf of moral imagination in regard to this function: these claims ascribe to moral imagination a power to represent our human likenesses in ways that make it possible for them to serve as a basis for human community. Moral imagination has, if you will, a transformative power with regard to these representations. It starts with the quite unpromising materials of the likenesses we have to each other in the world of what is; these are, most often, likenesses of vulnerability and need. A likeness of this kind can foster cooperation for attaining particular goals. Its power to foster the construction of the more extensive realm for shared human action that we can call community is more problematic. Philosophers in the tradition of social contract have made efforts to depict the human community that develops from recognition of human likeness of this kind. Their efforts, therefore, are particularly instructive for our consideration of the transformative power of moral imagination. Their arguments that cooperation is enjoined by the recognition of our human likeness in vulnerability and need are almost paradigmatically self-evident. How they then move from cooperation, which deals with these particular vulnerabilities and needs, to a community, which makes it possible to share human concerns beyond those of vulnerabilities and needs, is often not as straightforward argumentatively. This is so because human community frequently has to be envisioned as originating from, and fostering, a more extensive range of human likeness than can be represented just in the vulnerabilities and needs that first enjoined cooperation. The move from cooperation to community, save in the case in which community is conceived as serving only those needs that enjoined cooperation, requires, therefore, an exercise of imagination. This exercise of imagination is needed to depict how and why we go on to a more extensive sharing of human concerns from a starting place upon the narrow base of cooperation enjoined by needs.

This transformative power of moral imagination can also be characterized as our capacity to represent human likeness by reference to a moral future: when we represent our human likeness functioning as a basis for human community, we are not simply recording it as an element of the world of what is. Rather, the recognition "I am like her; she is like me" serves as a starting point for us then to go on together. We acknowledge our likeness now, but we also acknowledge it in function of our expectations for the future: our likeness to each other provides possibilities, both now and later, for our acting in common to give shape to the existence that we have acknowledged we share.

The connection of moral imagination with hope is located in this capability for referring our representations of human likeness to the moral future. This capability functions to open possibilities for our acting in common to give shape to the existence we acknowledge we share. The particular possibilities for acting in common that are opened for us will be determined in accord with the human likeness we have recognized and referred to the moral future. Thus, to the argument I have been constructing we now can pose this fundamental question: Upon the acknowledgment of the human likeness implied in the claim that history is the will of a just God who knows us, what hopes may we have for common action to give shape to the human existence that we share?

This question provides another formulation for the issues raised at the end of the last section. It makes those issues more tractable, however, inasmuch as it raises them first with reference to possibilities and, thereby, to hope, rather than to what is and, thereby, to truth. As our discussion will illustrate, that is the proper order in which to seek their resolution, because, for a world of what ought to be, that which is true turns upon that for which I may justly hope.

Before specifying the hope that may justly come to be upon acknowledgment of the likeness implied in the claim that history is the will of a just God who knows us, let me note the general pattern of possibilities opened up by acknowledgment of human likeness as the frame of a moral world. Moral theory has developed in the course of its history a number of terms that denote the forms of human likeness that can serve as the frame of a moral world: "nature," "will," "feeling," are among them. The acknowledgment of likeness conveyed by these terms, however, is not confined to the elements they represent in the world of what is. Thus, for instance, what the likeness of "human nature" represents, for purposes of the moral governance of conduct, is not merely a set of general facts from the world of what is that are true of all humans; it represents, in at least one tradition that employs the term, a set of fundamental possibilities for shaping human existence that arise in virtue of human ends and purposes.[23] Similarly, what the likeness denoted by "feeling" or "moral sentiment" represents, for the sake of the moral interpretation and governance of conduct, is not simply the sum total of instances of human fellow feeling and the conduct it has engendered; nor does it represent simply a prognosis for a general continuance of such instances. These terms represent, rather, a set of possibilities for shaping human existence in accord with the feelings that arise with the exercise of human reciprocity in a whole range of human activities.[24]

Human community is the term I propose to use to unify the possibilities opened up by acknowledgment of human likeness as the frame of a moral world. The particular form in which human community is envisioned will be in function of the human likeness that is taken to be basic for the frame of a moral world: the way I picture what makes me like you, and you like me, gives fundamental shape to the way I picture how we can all live well with each other. As a result, the question of what possibilities for common action follow from the acknowledgment of human likeness is also a question about the shape we hope to give to human community.[25] This latter question is most useful for the task of specifying more exactly the human likeness that is acknowledged in the claim that history is the will of a just God who knows us.

In virtue of this latter question, the human likeness acknowledged in this claim can be specified as follows: we stand together in relation to a transcendent God through the actions and dispositions that link us to the past — our own and each other's — and carry us from the present to the future — our own and each other's. The moral world for which this likeness is a frame is one that promises that such actions and dispositions will effect for us a full relationship to each other and to the transcendent God. In making such a promise, this moral world stands in sharp contrast to the world of what is: the actions that link us to the past and carry us from the present into the future constantly seem to fail in effecting for us, in the world of what is, a full relationship to one another, let alone to a transcendent God. In making this promise, such a moral world thus also brings about a disheartening recognition: it promises what we have been aroused to crave in the actions and dispositions that link us to each other — an enduring achievement of human community. Yet its very promise is a sign that this achievement is beyond the power of our unaided wit, will, and work to effect.

We can be aroused to crave enduring achievement of human community well before any explicit acknowledgment of this likeness in standing together before a transcendent God and placement of trust in the promise it makes. The concrete human communalities we most readily recognize in the world of what is are partial and particular. In serving to mark out likeness, they mark out unlikeness as well. In virtue of such communalities — be they of family, clan, tribe, language, race, or nation — we can say to some: "I am like you; you are like me"; in virtue of the same communalities, however, we can also say to others: "I am not like you; you are not like me." As partial and as particular as the communalities are, they are able, at times, to arouse in us a craving that there be likenesses by which we can identify with at least some who have fallen outside the scope of our acknowledged communalities. In one of its simplest forms, this craving is the desire to make of the stranger a friend.

This is, to be sure, a fitful desire. We can make much of certain communalities — for example, race, language, creed — precisely because they seem less likely to arouse this kind of desire in us. Despite careful efforts to delimit the bounds of such likeness, there can yet come a stranger who, though on the other side of these bounds, brings to mind a more inclusive likeness we may have forgotten or perhaps had not yet seen. The partial and particular character of our human communalities, moreover, almost ensures that there will be some to whom we become the strangers, even though we desire that this not be. In whatever form this craving takes — to make of the stranger a friend, to cease to be strangers ourselves — it opens for us the possibility of representing our human communality in ways that are more inclusive than the likeness we first acknowledged. In this craving is a deep root of the tales of welcoming the stranger.[26]

Even as we make our communality more inclusive, there nonetheless comes a partial recognition that the craving that has been aroused still lies beyond the power we have to satisfy it. We become aware that the human likenesses that promised to be more fully inclusive are not given to us that way; instead, we must strive to make what is given in the likeness more inclusive, even if this requires displacement of those partial communalities we relied upon to distinguish friend from stranger. This proves to be no easy task; we constantly find ourselves making parochial the communalities that have promised to be inclusive. Thus we work for particular goals and identify with those who strive with us for common goals; we remain indifferent to others who strive for different goals, or become actively hostile to them when their goals conflict with ours.

In the striving that we each and all undertake for our particular goals, we far too often leave for the consideration only of the philosopher the one fact that may be far more important for governing what we do than the achievement of any particular goal: the human communality that is manifest in our very striving toward goals. In a similar way, human communalities of will, of work, of intelligence, of feeling, can all be rendered into impotent abstractions if we fail to see them as empowering the capacities our particularities have for fostering the interdependence that enables us to go on together.[27]

Although we can envision various forms of human likeness as

pledges of the full achievement of human community, many of our practices for dealing with one another show that the reliance we place on such a pledge is small. We show this by shaping many of our practices upon those human likenesses that can offer no such pledge — for example, fear, contention, suspicion. Rather than pledging the full achievement of moral community, these likenesses presume that our interaction will be continually marked by the exploitation of human weaknesses. In accord with this presumption, we then find ourselves willing to settle our expectations upon far less than the full achievement of human community. We make small our desire for the moral future. All that we reasonably hope and strive for as the way of living well with one another are barriers sufficient to prevent certain exploitations of human weakness from destroying us all, as we each go our own way as best we can.

Hope: Communality Imaged for the Moral Future

To make the human communalities we acknowledge more inclusive, we must represent them not just as they are, but also as they ought to be. Representing them as they ought to be allows them to give shape to our expectations of the moral future. The images that Niebuhr suggests guide moral theory — artisan, citizen, responder — each give instance of this. Each of them represents a pattern of activity in the world of what is; yet each takes on a properly moral function by then offering a pattern upon which to form our expectations about conduct that is yet to be and about the appropriate outcome of such conduct. Thus, in virtue of the image of artisan, we envision possibilities that our conduct has for shaping elements of the world of what is into accord with human purposes. In virtue of the image of citizen, we expect an appropriate outcome of properly governed human conduct to be the maintenance and promotion of a just public order. In accord with the image of responder, we essay to shape our conduct to evoke responses from others that enable us all to acknowledge and to strengthen our interdependence.[28] By giving shape to our expectations about human conduct, images such as these provide us with concrete representations made in accord with a disposition that we may appropriately term "hope."

Hope arises with the acknowledgment of human likeness; it arises as a disposition toward the efficacy of our conduct for achieving the moral future that we envision. In its most general form, hope is the expectation that from the acknowledgment of our likeness, we can then act in ways that enable us to go on together. It is the expectation that whatever else our conduct accomplishes, it will also serve to continue our going on together, and, thus, bring us much closer to the enduring achievement of human community. Moral imagination gives this expectation concrete form: in accord with this likeness, we can go on together this way. Once I acknowledge you as like me, and myself as like you, we cannot deal with each other without taking into account our likeness. Precisely how we go on together and how we deal with each other will be a function of the particular likeness we have acknowledged. For instance, the community we can hope our conduct to effect in virtue of our likeness as artisan will differ in important respects from the one we can hope our conduct to effect in virtue of our likeness as citizen.

Hope carries forward the expectation for human community that can be aroused by our partial and merely particularistic human communalities. In carrying forward such expectations, hope bears upon human conduct in its movement from past to present, and from present to future. Hope, as made concrete through moral imagination, thereby takes on an essentially historical character.

The hope that the acknowledgment of human communality arouses is that our conduct has power to shape ways for us to go on together. Hope looks to the efficacy of our conduct for the moral future. As a result, it disposes us to expect our conduct to effect ways of going on together that are not yet actual in the world of what is; in particular, it disposes us to expect that such ways of going on together will be more inclusive, that they will make it possible for the stranger to become friend. Even though hope gives our expectations this form, we cannot deny that the power of our conduct to effect ways of going on together is far more ambiguous than hope would have it. The origin of this power lies in the recognition of communalities that are partial and particularistic. As a result, the ways of going on together that our conduct fashions can also take on a partial and particularistic character: "we" go on together, "they" do not — or, even more disappointing to hope — "they" may not, should not, go on together.

Hope: Recognition of the Finitude of Human Conduct

In noting this possibility of the disappointment of hope, we reach a crucial juncture in the argument I have been constructing. The ambiguity of the power of our conduct to effect ways of going on together suggests that hope, as I have characterized it, is doomed, in principle, to disappointment. No concrete human communality seems adequate to maintain our conduct in the hope that it can effect the full attainment of human community. The partial and particularistic character of the concrete human communalities we most readily acknowledge can be expanded to include more whom I am willing to acknowledge as "like me": where once I identified just with family or clan, I now can identify with tribe and nation; beyond tribe and nation I can identify with those beyond the limits of its communality who speak my tongue, worship as I do, labor as I do. Yet, as I try to identify with all in a common humanity, I appear to reach a limit. The hope that was aroused on the basis of a recognition of concrete ways in which I am like you comes to term far short of its goal of the full achievement of human community. Out of these communalities we have not effected the full attainment of human community; we have simply fashioned more inclusive representations of our human likeness — for example, human "nature," the human "family," the term "humanity" itself. These representations appear to be either abstractions or metaphors that lack full power to shape conduct in ways that can make it effective for the full attainment of human community. In fact, their abstract or metaphorical character can far too easily serve to make them useful masks for furthering divisive human particularities. All this suggests again that hope in the efficacy of human conduct for the full achievement of human community is doomed to disappointment.

Recognition of human communality is what first aroused this hope; that recognition was taken as a promise for the moral future. If hope is doomed to disappointment, it is because partial and particularistic human communalities appear too weak to support the promise. Hope is doomed to disappointment if the sole source from which it has been offered this promise lies in communalities that remain partial and only particularistic. There is, however, a communality that is prior to those that are partial and particularistic: it is a communality whose recognition can be ours in virtue of the telling and the hearing of human action in narrative; it is what I shall term the communality of our human finitude. Our human conduct remains incomplete until we have been enduringly bound together into a community. This communality, and this alone, offers a basis on which it becomes possible to maintain human conduct in the hope of full attainment of human community. In this communality is made manifest the incapacity of our wit, will, and work to effect such full attainment. As this communality is made manifest in narrative, however, such incapacity does not signal the end of hope, but rather it points us toward a source from which to long for and to expect its satisfaction.

Narrative, by its very form, exhibits this communality to us; it exhibits the finitude of human conduct and the anticipation of its completion. It does so by serving, in the telling and the hearing, as a sign effecting what we hope for: it makes present a moment of the enduring attainment of human community. It does so by means of an irony that to reason appears paradoxical, but to faith shows God's loving humor: tales that tell of how human community based solely upon the recognition of partial communalities is confounded: in the presence of unconditioned trust, fidelity, or innocence; in the face of loss, tedium, pain, and even death.

One thinks of Tolstoy's *The Death of Ivan Ilych*. Faced with Ivan's dying, his friends, co-workers, and family can no longer sustain the communalities that once bound them together to Ivan. The simple compassion of a servant to ease his pain, however, enables a going on together that sustains him into his death. The final going on together of Ivan and his servant, moreover, though brief both in time and in telling—and itself a most clear sign of human finitude—provides a glimpse of what must be present for there to be any enduring to our goings on together. This narrative, therefore, exhibits the communality of our finitude as a sign of the possibility of enduring community. It does so not just in the content of the tale it tells; it does so as well simply by entrusting the tale to our hearing, for it to be a moment of identity with the communality Ivan and his servant exhibit, for us to cherish that moment of identity and then hand it on to others. In being so entrusted to us and thus itself exhibiting the dependence that is a mark of finitude, a tale such as this shows narrative's own proper power: it enables imagination to sustain us for the future. Narrative is, thereby, an effective sign of a power to endure, not of our own devising, that must be given to our goings on together, if they are to proceed in hope.

The hope that narrative has the power to engender is not doomed to disappointment, because this hope does not rest solely upon those partial and merely particularistic human communalities that prove unable to effect the full attainment of human community. The hope that narrative engenders is not just what we can imagine the attainment of human community to be, by our own wit, will, and work. Narrative engenders, rather, a hope that the full attainment of human community will be far beyond what we could imagine, will, or work for. Narrative engenders this hope because in it we are made susceptible to being touched by history as it is the will of a just God who knows us.

Narrative: The Transformation of Finitude to the Service of Mutuality

The way in which narrative makes us susceptible to being touched by history will be examined in greater detail in chapter 4. At this stage of my argument, all we need note is the singular context that narrative provides for the recognition of human likeness: it gathers us together to tell and to hear of what men and women once did, or what they might have done, in the anticipation that, whatever the particular tale, whether it happened just thus and so or not, such deeds hold forth for each of us some moment of recognition of our identity with one another. Narrative presents human conduct as it is concretely limited, by time, place, and all manner of human circumstance; yet in the telling and the retelling there is a transformation. The deeds do not shed their limitations; they remain finite, limited human actions. Yet the telling and the retelling give the deeds a further and necessary completion of their human character. They are no longer just the actions of solitary individuals, once upon a time; they can now become an abiding part of the moral world — the world framed by the acknowledgment of human communality — of each and all who hear them.

The finitude of human conduct that narrative exhibits is thereby its need for completion in human mutuality and solidarity. It is a "moral" finitude in that it has its origin in a recognition of human communality. Narrative enables us to see that this moral finitude of human conduct does not lie in failure to accomplish fully its particular intended effect, nor in failure to instance a norm of action. A tale with a happy ending and a tale of moral courage both represent such accomplishments, yet the accomplishment is not enough for the moral completion of the deed. The deed demands telling and retelling so that it can continue to serve to effect in some way the attainment of human community. Narrative presents to us deeds with the power to elicit a mutuality in telling and hearing: we would have it told this way, for this says who we are.

Narrative thereby provides a context in which human deeds can be brought to completion by being set in explicit service to the recognition of human mutuality. In consequence, narrative also illuminates the moral character of the deeds we undertake: they are to be such that, whatever their limitations, whatever other human purposes they serve, they can be brought to completion by being set in explicit service to the recognition of human mutuality. Our deeds must be such that they too can become a part of the moral world of each who hear of them. They enable those who hear of them to say: we would have it told what you have done, for these deeds help make it plain that we are like to each other and that we are bound to each other.

Narrative provides the context in which we can recognize the more inclusive human communality of the moral finitude of our conduct. It provides, as well, a moment in which that finitude, though remaining in its particularity, is partially transcended: deeds undertaken upon recognition just of our partial communalities, no matter how divisive and destructive of possibilities of going on together they were in execution, become, in the telling and listening, occasions for the recognition of that likeness from which we can always go on.[29] By providing these moments, narrative engenders hope. Hope takes the form of seeing these moments as signs of the presence of the full achievement of human community. In hope, we see these moments enabling us to measure our achievement in going on together: if much, to rejoice, yet to seek to go on further; if little, to mourn, yet to start anew.

The presence of these moments, however, does not seem sufficient to provide a guarantee of hope's most longed for object: that our conduct will succeed in effecting enduring attainment of human community. The fitful, symbolic presence found in narrative may well be all we are to have; the hope that narrative engenders seems far from sure. We will always consider it far from sure if we are forgetful of an important fact: it is the sureness proper to a world of what ought to be. In such a world, a hope that is sure can have its ground only in freedom. My argument therefore must now take a turn to explore human freedom. What must be shown is that the hope engendered by narrative is sure because through it we are enabled to represent the destiny to which we are called in the exercise of our freedom.

3. Sure Hope

I. HUMAN DESTINY AND MORAL FREEDOM

Freedom: The Service of Human Mutuality

The acknowledgment that I am like you and that you are like me fosters expectations that we can and will go on together. In this simple way, hope in the attainment of human community arises from the recognition of human likeness. Although there are many forms of human likeness, the argument developed in the preceding chapter proposes that we consider one of these forms — our likeness in the finitude of our conduct — as the basis on which we can most appropriately hope for the full achievement of human community. It also presents narrative as particularly suited to exhibit to us this likeness: the tale of human deeds has power to make this likeness present to us as a promise of the enduring attainment of human community.

There is, as I have already noted, an air of paradox to this claim that the finitude of our conduct — that is, its inability to effect the abiding attainment of human community that the recognition of our likeness to each other promises — serves, nonetheless, as the very basis on which we can hope for such attainment. This chapter presents what I take to be a partial resolution of this paradox: this resolution is based upon the case that can be made, on philosophical grounds, for understanding human freedom as essentially ordered to mutuality. Once this case is made, moreover, it will then be possible to move my argument, in chapter 4, to the theological grounds that offer the basis for a more complete resolution of this paradox. These grounds will

81

be provided by the acknowledgment, which faith makes possible, of God's transcendence as the power upon which we can and, indeed, must rely to bring about the abiding attainment of human community.

I shall develop my case for the ordering of freedom to mutuality, and for the appropriateness of the subsequent move to theological considerations, from a source that, in the judgment of much of contemporary philosophy, would appear to offer little in its support: Kant's discussions of human moral freedom and of its bearings on the possibility of a philosophically justifiable human acknowledgment of the reality of a transcendent God.[1] The reasons why Kant's discussions are judged to be such an unpromising source of support are quite complex. The case I shall present in this chapter focuses only upon the one I consider most important: the interpretation that much contemporary philosophy has commonly given Kant's account of human moral autonomy. That interpretation is of a piece with what I termed, at the beginning of this work, the fundamental mistake of our contemporary self-understanding of freedom: we conceive of freedom primarily, if not exclusively, in reference to human agents in their individuality and independence, rather than in terms of their shared human communalities and their fundamental interdependence. Kant's work — most particularly, his moral philosophy — is quite commonly, and, I suspect, quite mistakenly, interpreted as a seminal intellectual rendering of such self-understanding.[2]

I consider a discussion of Kant's account of moral autonomy to be particularly useful for the project of establishing a philosophical foundation for the enterprise of moral theology. This is so because this account, once it is properly understood in terms of the mutuality that Kant acknowledges as the term of the exercise of human freedom, presents a picture of human conduct that faith can take into its ambit of understanding. Kant's account of human moral conduct provides a basis on which we can relate the freedom that characterizes human moral endeavor to the freedom that is enabled by faith's assent to God. As Kant's account has been most commonly interpreted, however, no such relationship seems possible. Put in simple terms, the core features of Kant's account have frequently been taken to render assent to a transcendent God at least unnecessary, if not, in fact, both theoretically and practically meaningless.

In the course of this chapter I propose to show that there are reasons to think that this interpretation neither adequately nor accurately represents Kant's view. These reasons will be drawn from an examination of Kant's discussions of "hope," "the highest good," and reason's "interest" that takes its most fundamental form as "moral faith." The reasons to be drawn from such an examination, moreover, are important not only because they cast doubt upon standard readings of Kant; they are important also because they provide for us one perspective from which we can gain a clear sight upon the essential ordering of freedom to mutuality: they provide us with the perspective of the future. It is from this perspective, moreover, that we shall also begin to note the appropriateness of then moving to theological considerations in order to give a more adequate account of the ordering of freedom to mutuality. It is from the perspective of the future promised by the exercise of freedom that our gaze can be drawn to catch sight of this possibility: God's own mutuality stands as the source that has gifted human freedom with its ordering to mutuality, and gives trustworthy assurance of its completion in the abiding attainment of community.

Kant's Question of Hope: The Power of Freedom to Attain Good

My discussion of Kant's account of human moral autonomy begins at an unusual place: the reasons he offers, after apparently completing his analysis of human moral conduct in terms of autonomy, for raising the question: What may I hope?[3] These reasons will indicate that he did conceive human freedom to be essentially ordered to the service of human mutuality. This ordering is made evident in the concern for a shared human destiny to which freedom gives voice in the question: What may I hope?

In Kant's view, this concern for human destiny does not arise from mere chance or curiosity. It arises, rather, because the exercise of freedom in human conduct makes us pose the question of hope in terms that can be satisfied only by the accomplishment of a shared, common human destiny. Thus, the connection Kant makes between the exercise of freedom in human conduct and the origin of hope will provide a basis for understanding freedom as essentially ordered to the service of mutuality. This connection is made most clearly in Kant's discussions of the object of the hope to which freedom gives rise; Kant designates this object as "the highest good."[4] The specification he gives to the highest good indicates the ordering of freedom to mutuality: the hope to which the exercise of my freedom gives rise is that my conduct will effect the attainment of abiding good, not for myself alone, but for each and all who exercise freedom.

Kant's discussion of the highest good makes it clear that, even though the question of hope is formulated as singular and personal, it is, nonetheless, more fundamentally about a common and shared human destiny. Kant does not doubt that the singular and personal good that freedom gives me hope of attaining can be conceived only as the satisfaction of my human cravings. But his account of hope clearly places the attainment of my singular and personal good in the context of a moral future constituted by the title we each and all can claim to membership in an abiding moral community. There are a number of texts that can be cited in support of this view that we understand Kant's account of the highest good to have its focus upon the shared and interconnected character of the human destiny that is to be ours in virtue of the morally autonomous exercise of our freedom. One text in which Kant indicates that such is the focus of his understanding of the highest good comes, significantly, from a section in the *Critique of Practical Reason*, in which he identifies his critically expounded concept of the highest good with the Christian doctrine of the attainment of the kingdom of God:

> But the moral law does not of itself promise happiness, for the latter is not, according to concepts of any order of nature, necessarily connected with obedience to the law. Christian ethics supplies this defect of the second indispensable component of the highest good by *presenting a world* wherein reasonable beings single-mindedly devote themselves to the moral law; this is the Kingdom of God, in which nature and morality come into a harmony, which is foreign to each as such, through a holy Author of the world, who makes possible the derived highest good [italics added].[5]

This focus is made even clearer in a passage from the *Lectures on Philosophical Theology*:

> But if he is conscious of following his duty, then a man is certain of being a member or link in the chain of the kingdom

of ends. This thought gives him comfort and reassurance. It makes him inwardly noble and worthy of happiness. And *it raises him to the hope that he may constitute a whole together with all other rational beings in the kingdom of morals*, in just the same way that everything is connected and unified in the kingdom of nature. Now man has a secure foundation on which to build his faith in God [italics added].[6]

Another way Kant indicates that human freedom, exercised in moral autonomy, is ordered to mutuality is in the claim that the exercise of freedom puts us into an intelligible "world" — into a connected and ordered totality of relationships to the moral agency of each and all who constitute human moral community.[7] Kant provides a description, in *Religion within the Limits of Reason Alone*, of the process of making moral judgments. This description suggests one way in which he takes this process to be a function of our capability for representing an interconnected world of human agents shaping their conduct through the exercise of freedom:

Take a man who, honoring the moral law, allows the thought to occur to him (he can scarcely avoid doing so) of what sort of a world he would create, under the guidance of practical reason, were such a thing in his power, a world into which, moreover, he would place himself as a member. He would not merely make the very choice which is determined by the moral idea of the highest good, were he vouchsafed solely the right to choose; he would also will that [such] a world should by all means come into existence (because the moral law demands that the highest good possible by our agency should be realized) and he would will so even though, in accordance with this idea, he saw himself in danger of paying in his own person a heavy price in happiness — it being possible that he might not be adequate to the [moral] demands of the idea, demands which reason lays down as conditioning happiness. Accordingly he would feel compelled by reason to avow this judgment with complete impartiality, as though it were rendered by another and yet, at the same time, as his own; whereby man gives evidence of the need, morally effected in him, of also conceiving a final end for his duties, as their consequence.[8]

Our freedom, as Kant here describes its exercise in moral de-
cisions, functions to place us in a world constituted in its moral
character by relationships of mutuality. These relationships are
of a particular kind: they are the ones that make it possible for
persons to render impartial judgment upon one another's conduct. It is particularly important to note that these relationships
of mutuality do not have as a prior condition an acknowledgment by individual moral agents just of their own freedom, as
if it were grounded independently of the mutual acknowledgment of human freedom that is effectively rendered by submitting to such impartial judgment. Such a prior condition would
seriously misconstrue the character of freedom; it would keep
us from seeing that the acknowledgment I make of my own freedom can take place only in the context of the mutual acknowledgment of freedom that is a constitutive element of moral
community.

There is a picture of human freedom that denies it this character of mutual acknowledgment — the human agent in lofty and
lonely moral solitude at the moment of decision. As I have pointed
out above, this picture has been mistakenly attributed to Kant.
If attention is paid to the connection Kant makes between human
freedom and the hope such freedom engenders in human destiny, then the correct picture emerges: the exercise of human freedom in a moral decision to shape conduct is our precise point
of contact with one another in mutuality, and it promises us full
participation in human community.

The passages I have cited are not the only ones in which Kant
indicates that freedom, particularly when it is viewed as the
ground for hope, is ordered to the fostering and attainment of
mutuality. There are, for instance, the discussions in which Kant
uses terms that presuppose that there is a shared and interconnected character to the prospect that is opened up to us by the
exercise of freedom — a "world" or a "kingdom" of which we find
ourselves members.[9] It is in virtue of this participation in a shared
world, which is constituted in and by human freedom in human
action, that the "interest," of reason made manifest in the exercise of freedom, gains its focus upon human destiny. This prospect and this focus do not seem to open up for the agent whose
moral autonomy is pictured as the loneliness of the moment of
moral choice. As Kant himself conceives of the hope that has its

focus on the highest good, however, its origin cannot be in the freedom exercised in virtue of such solitary moral agency; its origin can be only in the exercise of a freedom ordered to the fostering and attainment of mutuality.

The Moral Future and the Images of Freedom

Although Kant makes it quite clear that hope has its origin in freedom, commentators have only recently started to note that the freedom that gives rise to this hope must be ordered to mutuality.[10] The picture that Kant provides of the moral future through his concept of the highest good and his doctrine of hope is that of the full attainment of human community. He speaks of this community in images that make clear its public and shared character: a "kingdom of ends," an "ethical commonwealth," even a "kingdom of grace."[11] Kant's account of the highest good indicates that he sees this future as possible only insofar as our conduct is shaped through the exercise of freedom that keeps the attainment of mutuality continually in view.

It is this picture of the moral future, framed by the concept of the highest good and the doctrine of hope, that requires revision of the long-standing image of human freedom usually attributed to Kant: the solitary individual who takes upon herself or himself the full burden of responsibility for making moral choices. Revision of this image is not a matter of interest to scholars alone: this image has profoundly shaped Western moral thinking and practice for almost two centuries. Revision can take place from the perspective of mutuality that a concept such as the highest good provides: acknowledgment of and participation in a moral community of persons is a presupposition both for the exercise of freedom and for rendering an intelligible account of such exercise. Kant's account of freedom as it is exercised by human moral agents is unintelligible apart from this presupposition.

Kant's account of hope in the attainment of the highest good is one way of making manifest the ordering of freedom to mutuality. The focus of this account upon the shared and interconnected character of the highest good, moreover, places upon our moral thinking a requirement that initially may seem both arcane and abstract: our representations of the highest good must show it to be such that each and every moral agent can share in it, and that in it the outcomes of the moral conduct of each and all can be brought into full and ordered connection with one another. This requirement may seem less arcane and abstract, however, if we consider it to be a reminder that, if our freedom is essentially ordered to mutuality, then both our moral thinking and our moral conduct are fundamentally matters of the public realm.

By putting the point of Kant's account of the highest good this way, I am deliberately making it into a challenge to the correctness of what has come to be a truism for our culture: that moral thinking and moral conduct are paradigmatically private matters. What makes it plausible to consider them private matters is, of course, the image of solitary moral agency. If we break the spell of that image, however, we must then be ready to consider the possibility that, in virtue of its ordering to mutuality, our freedom as moral agents has been given, as one of its primary moral exercises, the charge to fashion and sustain a public realm in which each and all can attain good.[12]

I believe it is important to point out that the claim I am making — that moral thinking and moral conduct are matters of the public realm — is not directly a claim about the relationship between morality and law. It is a claim, however, that might prove to be of use for locating what has gone amiss in many recent efforts in our culture to come to grips, both theoretically and practically, with issues that have been posed in terms of the relationship between morality and law. To say that, in accord with Kant's account of the highest good, moral thinking and moral conduct are matters of the public realm is to say that, in consequence of our destiny to share in an abiding good, they are such that we can be held accountable to one another for them. The conceptual focus of such accountability is upon our understanding of good and upon the shape we give to our conduct in accord with that understanding. We can effectively hold one another to such accountability, moreover, only if we are willing to address directly the question of the forms our life with one another in a community ought to take. We must ask of ourselves what kind of public realm, what form of commonwealth, are we willing to work with one another to fashion, to sustain, and to entrust to the future. We need in each generation, an effort to reflect upon the very nature of public order and of our political commitment to one another — that is, the commitment we have to each other in virtue of being members of the same public, political realm, the same *polis*.[13]

Many of our society's recent efforts to deal with issues posed in terms of the relationship between morality and law — for example, human rights, the termination of life, pornography, abortion — have had less than satisfactory resolution in consequence of our failure to face more fundamental questions of the nature of public order and of our political commitment to one another. We — whether our political labels are liberal, moderate, or conservative — have let these questions be settled by accepting, in practice, the presupposition that the responsibility for sustaining the public order and the conditions of our political commitment to one another rest solely upon the institutions of government. We have come to regard more and more of our other institutions and practices — for example, the professions, the academic world, the arts, commerce, the churches, the customs of civility and public decorum — as instruments principally of the promotion of particular interests. As a result of this bifurcation, we have been increasingly unable to sustain, for any of these latter institutions, an effective role in holding us publicly accountable to one another. We thus, not surprisingly, find ourselves in circumstances in which it becomes increasingly difficult to appeal to anything but law as an instrument of public accountability. Here we have, once more, a set of circumstances that point to the condition I designated in chapter 1 as the fragmentation of the public realm.

My purpose in taking note of this issue in the context of Kant's discussion of hope and of the highest good is to suggest where we might find the conceptual tools for its resolution. There is little possibility for its resolution, either in general terms, or in regard to particular matters — whether they are questions of human rights, abortion, pornography, corporate practices, or the conduct of government officials and agencies — unless we are willing to formulate and address the far more fundamental questions of the nature of the public realm that we are willing to work with one another to fashion and to sustain. Kant's discussion of hope and of the highest good, moreover, has a particular relevance to such discussion. It helps us locate some of the lines of thinking that we must pursue in order to initiate and to sustain discussion of such questions.

A brief consideration of one such line of thinking seems in order before turning back to a discussion of other elements of Kant's account of hope and the highest good that are of consequence for the foundation of moral theology. Kant's account of hope urges us to pursue a line of thinking that would lead us to examine certain items we uncritically assume in the judgment we make about our own good, be it as individuals or as a group. Kant's account suggests that our judgments about such good can be considered morally adequate only if that good can be shown to be at least in harmony with, if not actually contributory to, the totality of good for each and for all. Put more simply, Kant's discussion suggests that there is something morally amiss at a very deep level with justifications offered in support of courses of action that come to an end with some form of the appeal that "It's good for me," or that "It's in our best interests." The presumption of such an appeal is a claim to privileged knowledge: who better to judge what is good for us, or in our own best interests, than we who are pressing the claim? Kant's account suggests something quite different: something can truly be good for me, or in our best interests, only if its good can at least be put in harmony with what is to be good in some enduring way for others.

If individuals and groups were to follow this line of thinking, it would provide a basis for their making a critical assessment of what they hitherto pressed as a privileged claim to know best what is good for them or in their interests. Such a critical evaluation can be made, however, by engaging in that exercise of moral reasoning that is most difficult because it requires imaginative detachment from the very interest whose claim one is pressing. Such an imaginative detachment is a discipline to which we do not readily submit, particularly when pressing claims in the public realm. We allow, instead, the function of critical evaluation to fall upon the adversative forms we have increasingly let the institutions of the public realm take: If anyone is to challenge the interest we press for the adequacy of its claim to good, let it be others who do so, in virtue of their own interests, but not ourselves. Claims made in terms of rights seem particularly susceptible to being pressed in this fashion. We do not seem particularly willing to ask of ourselves what good, or whose good, other than our own, is served either by our having a certain power as a matter of right, or by our exercise of that power.

In circumstances in which claims to rights are pressed without due critical attention to the relationship such rights and their exercise bear to the attainment of good for each and all, there results a narrowing of the moral world: pressing a claim to rights allows us to withdraw, now this, now that area of our conduct from accountability to one another. Once we have withdrawn our conduct from such accountability, we are then committed to forms of moral thinking that make it impossible for us to represent the appropriate completion of all human moral action — that is, the highest good — as the attainment of an abiding good that is shareable by each and by all. By withdrawing our conduct from such accountability, we effectively claim that it is of no interest to us how that conduct and its outcome bear upon the attainment of good for each and for all. As we shall see in chapter 5, such withdrawal from public accountability to one another, save that defined in law, has wrought its consequences upon areas such as marriage, the family, and the professions. We have allowed the practices that give shape to these human activities — and others as well — to take focus upon the promotion of a good that is understood to be particular, private, and immediate, rather than common, shareable, and enduring.

Mutuality: Reason's Construction of a Moral World

We should not find it surprising that Kant characterizes the prospect opened for us by the exercise of freedom in terms that are far different from those presupposed by the contemporary practice of pressing numerous claims in terms of rights. For Kant that prospect is not one of a set of heterogeneous goods, discretely satisfying a set of individuals; it is a prospect of unified and unifying good, shared among persons linked with one another in the form of a community. This prospect is in keeping with his understanding of freedom in its practical (moral) use. For Kant, reason is "world-constructing": our human efforts to represent totality bear the stamp of reason.[14] The question "What may I hope?" arises because there is an opaqueness about the moral efficacy of freedom as it gives shape to human conduct. This opacity does not concern our possession or exercise of freedom; rather, the opacity that causes the question of hope to emerge has as its background the very sureness we have of being free. Kant formulates this opacity as a question: What is to result from this right conduct of ours?[15] This question arises because reason's interest in totality cannot leave it unsettled whether or not the outcome of our conduct is ever to constitute a coherent totality of good, either for ourselves individually, or for all of us in the course of human history:

> Therefore it cannot be a matter of unconcern to morality as to whether or not it forms for itself the concept of a final end for all things (harmony with which while not multiplying men's duties, yet provides them with a special point of focus for the unification of all ends); for only thereby can objective, practical reality be given to the unity of the purposiveness arising from freedom with the purposiveness of nature, a union with which we cannot possibly dispense.[16]

Such concern for the outcome of our moral conduct is possible only if we are sure of our capability for acting, or for failing to act, morally. According to Kant we have this sureness; it is given to us as a "fact" in and through awareness of reason's moral demands that the exercise of freedom gives us.[17] This awareness is ours whenever we find ourselves in situations — or can imagine ourselves in situations — in which what we ought to do (e.g., not swear falsely, keep our promise, etc.) is clear and in which we are sure that we can do what ought to be done. The sureness that we can do what we ought, however, does not provide sureness that we will do it, nor about all that will come about, for good or for ill, from our doing as we ought.[18]

The question "What may I hope?" is thereby presented by Kant as one that arises from reason's "interest" in the efficacy of human moral conduct for attaining a totality of good. Reason takes this interest in the efficacy of human moral conduct because, in its guise as freedom — that is, as practical reason — it gives moral shape to human conduct. Reason's interest, Kant goes on to say, is satisfied in this case by the representation of the "highest good." This representation of the attainment of abiding good for each and all in and through relationships of mutuality is the appropriate object upon which a hope arising from reason's interest in totality can take its focus.

This shared and interconnected character of the highest good can be considered to constitute one feature that is fundamental to Kant's perspective upon the moral future. That future consists of the possibility and the sure promise of our constituting, through the exercise of human moral freedom, a world in which we each and all share in the full measure of good. That good, moreover, is the abiding satisfaction of our human cravings that can be effected by the human conduct in which freedom is exercised for the promotion of good for each and for all. We can designate this good as "human destiny": the representation of the outcome of our conduct as an abiding, interconnected totality brought to focus through our acknowledgment of our human likeness. As Kant presents his account of the moral future, the acknowledgment of our likeness in the finitude of our conduct provides his understanding of human destiny with a focus that enables him to depict the roles that freedom and our human cravings play in the attainment of that destiny. Those roles are, not surprisingly, quite different from what they have frequently been taken to be when portrayed in accord with the picture of autonomous and solitary moral agency. The remainder of this chapter will follow Kant as he traces the role of freedom to its limit. That limit is reached when freedom is seen to be itself a fundamental form of human craving.

Kant correctly sees that, though it is beyond the power of the concepts of his critical philosophy to account for freedom as a form of human craving, this particular character of freedom provides the basis for assent to the reality of God. From the considerations he offers in regard to the possibility and necessity of such assent, I shall develop my case for the appropriateness of moving to theological grounds to provide an account of freedom as a form of human craving. Those grounds will then be explored in detail in chapter 4, in which freedom will be exhibited as nothing less than the form of our most fundamental human craving: for mutuality. As such a craving, it images the reality of the God who gifted us with this craving so that we might be further gifted by its fulfillment, found in the mutuality that is participation in the very life of God. The task of providing an account of freedom's role at the foundation of the enterprise of moral theology will be completed once freedom is shown — by its very ordering to mutuality — to image the God who gifted us with this craving. The task will be complete when, as image of the gifting God, freedom can be seen to be both origin and term of moral theology's quest: freedom, ventured upon the quest for understanding and for rightly governing human conduct, is rendered open, by its ordering to mutuality, to quest for God.

II. HUMAN LIKENESS AND THE INTERESTS OF REASON

The Origins of Hope: Human Likeness and Human Freedom

In chapter 2, the acknowledgment of human likeness is presented as the origin of hope. Such hope has its focus upon the full attainment of human community. From the acknowledgment "I am like her; she is like me" arises the possibility of "going on together." Although the acknowledgment of human likeness is the source of hope, the particular likenesses upon which we try to go on together do not allow the hope they engender to be fully satisfied. There is, however, one likeness whose acknowledgment, particularly in the context of narrative, allows hope for the full attainment of human community to be sustained: even though other human likenesses reach limits in their capacity to sustain us in going on together, the human likeness that narrative manifests — the moral finitude of our conduct — can be transformed in the context of narrative into a source for sustaining hope. In the context of narrative, all the deeds and all the conduct we recount serve to effect in us a recognition of how thorough is our likeness to one another. Narrative sustains hope in our going on together by reminding us that it is the most fundamental human possibility; if we do not go on together, we each shall have nowhere to go, and going on alone will make no sense.

In this chapter, the sketch I have presented so far of Kant's doctrine of hope appears to provide it with a different origin — namely, in the exercise of human freedom. Such a difference is only apparent, however. The hope that has its origin in freedom has its focus on the efficacy of human conduct for attaining what Kant terms the "highest good." The good so attained is, for each and all, connected in abiding moral community and thus stands as the completion of our acknowledgment of human likeness. Kant's account of the highest good places it in the moral future: it is the abiding satisfaction of our human cravings insofar as this can be effected by the exercise of human freedom. The moral future, envisioned in accord with this concept of the highest good, also bears the stamp of the acknowledgment of our likeness: it is a public realm, shared by all who have gained title to membership in this realm by the exercise of their freedom. Kant's discussion of the role of freedom in effecting the moral future makes it clear that freedom is not just choice; it is also, and more fundamentally, craving. The focus of its craving, moreover, is one that his picture of the moral future as a public realm shows to be not the independence of the autonomous agent, but the abiding mutuality of a community of agents sharing in the totality of human good.

Kant's Vision of the Moral Future: Two Pictures

The most commonly accepted interpretations of Kant's account of the highest good, not surprisingly, have been shaped by an understanding of Kant's account of freedom in which the individual autonomous agent stands alone on stage. This has an ironic result: the moral future in which all have an abiding share in a common human destiny, which Kant himself took to be sure on the basis of its origin in freedom, has been rendered highly problematic for us, in both its content and its surety, by his interpreters. When Kant's interpreters picture freedom solely as the exercise of an individual's power of choice, they sever the link, central to Kant's account of hope, between human freedom and a shared human destiny. They sever this link inasmuch as freedom pictured in this way need not function for the attainment of such a destiny. In fact, when the freedom of the individual autonomous agent is pictured to be, most fundamentally, the power to choose among the varied objects of human cravings, it becomes problematic whether or not the exercise of freedom could effect the abiding satisfaction of the human cravings of even a single individual, let alone the human cravings of all who can be envisioned as members of an enduring ethical commonwealth or kingdom of ends. The power of freedom to shape our cravings and to bring them to satisfaction is limited to the extent that particular cravings have sources — for example, in physiological or cultural conditions — that we are not individually able to determine for ourselves. We thus often find ourselves in the grip of certain cravings — be they for food, or for honor, or for success — long before we acquire a knack for giving our cravings particular or sustained direction or for putting them in order when they crowd together upon us. Even when we acquire such a knack, it serves, at best, as an imperfect instrument for attaining an enduring satisfaction for our entire set of cravings.

Kant's account of the moral future, as the abiding satisfaction of the human cravings of each and all connected with one another in an enduring moral community, does not rest, however, on this picture of human freedom as principally the power of choice among the objects of our cravings. In order to attain human destiny in the form Kant envisions it, freedom must be the power that enables us to place our human likenesses and our particularities in service of the task of an enduring going on together. The exercise of an individual's power of choice, however, cannot provide such power in any sufficiency. The power of choice does not require that we take our going on together as anything but another object of choice. It allows us to picture the world as a mere aggregate of items that the exercise of freedom is to divide and parcel out at the service of each individual's cravings, rather than a totality to be formed by common action. According to this picture of freedom, we must frame our representation of the world through a focus upon the capacity of freedom, as the power of choice, to attain those objects that satisfy the cravings of each individual. When we represent the world through this focus, we set freedom upon a task that is in direct contrast to Kant's vision of the moral future: we set it to place the world at the service of human cravings. Kant's vision of the moral future sets freedom to a quite different task: to put our human cravings at the service of the endeavor to fashion a fully shared world.

As we shall see in the next chapter, such a picture of freedom fails to note the character that human cravings have as "gift." This gifted character has its origin in the ordering of freedom to mutuality. Awareness of the gifted character of human cravings enables us to take responsibility for shaping them so that our fulfillment of these cravings will be the fashioning and fostering of human mutuality. In shaping our cravings to the service of mutuality we are exercising what we may appropriately call the freedom of human moral endeavor. The mutuality we make present to one another in such moral endeavor makes it possible for freedom to function at the foundation of moral theology: our mutuality provides an effective sign of the presence of God's mutuality. From the perspective of moral theology, the mutuality we acknowledge in the freedom of moral endeavor invites us to respond in the freedom of faith: to accept this further, still more fundamental call to share in the mutuality of God's own life.

Kant's Account of Freedom: Reason's Interest in Mutuality

We need not, contrary to many of Kant's interpreters, render problematic his vision of the moral future as the possibility of constituting, through the exercise of human freedom, a world in which we each and all share a human destiny in full measure. We need not do so, because, as our consideration of reason's "interest" will now show, Kant did not take the exercise of an individual's power of choice to be the primary form of human freedom.

Kant did not conceive of the human freedom exercised in moral autonomy to take as its primary form the exercise of the individual's power of choice, because that power of choice does not offer an adequate ground on which we can base hope for the attainment of a shared human destiny. For the power of choice to be effective for the task of attaining a shared human destiny, it must be exercised under a condition that has its origin in that form of freedom that Kant does take to be primary— namely, in our capacity to acknowledge our fundamental human mutuality in the shape we give our conduct. Freedom, understood in this form, provides a condition basic to the sharing of any human good, let alone the all-inclusive good of human destiny. It is a condition that cannot have its basis in an individual's power of choice. This condition is that the interest I have in the possession and the exercise of my own freedom must be, as well, inherently an interest in the possession and the exercise of freedom by each and by all. The power of choice, it is true, *can be made to take such an interest.*[19] As Kant understands freedom, however, this is not an interest that freedom must be made to take; it is an interest that is already inherent in each exercise of freedom, even though we may not, and do not, always acknowledge it.

Kant's vision of the moral future, ironically, is rendered problematic by interpretations that fail to see that his discussions of reason's interest preclude making an individual's power of choice the fundamental form of human freedom. If, in fact, we understand freedom to take its fundamental form as an individual's power of choice, we will then be misled in our efforts to deal with a question that, from the perspective of Kant's account of reason's interest, is fundamentally easy to answer: What reasons are there for one free person to acknowledge the freedom of another? Our efforts to deal with this question will prove misleading because, according to the understanding of freedom as an individual's power of choice, there are no clear reasons inherent to "freedom" itself — that is, to my power to choose — that require me to take other persons' "freedom" — that is, their power to choose — into account. The reasons that might provide a satisfactory answer to this question, moreover, need not have their basis in considerations that give the power to choose an intrinsic human weight and value — that is, my acknowledgment of your power to choose need not be based on the fact that I value this power, regardless of who exercises it. I may offer such acknowledgment out of the tactical consideration that it may give my power to choose wider scope for its exercise.

Once this question of the grounds for acknowledgment of another's freedom is raised in terms of the belief that the primary form of freedom is the exercise of an individual's power of choice, it will prove difficult to find a conceptually adequate alternative to the view that moral conduct is, in fact, a sophisticated form of self-interested behavior and that moral theory functions to show how such self-interested behavior can be considered "enlightened" or "rational." Once the question is raised in these terms, moreover, we cannot begin to think of the possibility of a shared human destiny, let alone hope to attain it through the exercise of freedom. We cannot do so unless we can show that acknowledgment of another's freedom has a basis that is more fundamental than one provided by considerations that, because they ultimately reduce to enlightened self-interest, leave in question the inherent worth of a freedom possessed and exercised by one other than myself.

Kant's discussion of reason's interest indicates why we are misled in efforts to resolve this question when it is posed in terms that understand freedom to take its primary form as the individual's power to choose.[20] We are misled because this way of understanding freedom requires us to seek a more basic ground for that which, by virtue of its being an interest of reason, is already most basic for our understanding and for our action: in this case, it is seeking a more basic ground for freedom's interest in the promotion of freedom. Yet more basic grounds cannot be given, because this interest is already the most basic ground we have to offer in explicating what the exercise of our freedom requires of us — that is, the acknowledgment of each other's freedom. To ask for reasons that require one person to acknowledge the freedom of another — once we have identified this acknowledgment as a requirement of the very interest that freedom must exhibit as an exercise of reason — is to miss the whole point of Kant's account of freedom: its ordering to mutuality.

Moral philosophers are not the only ones who may be misled by the effort to answer, in terms of the individual's power of choice, the question: What reasons are there for one free person to acknowledge the freedom of another? There is, indeed, a sense in which efforts to resolve this question in terms of the power of choice have become the focus of our society's efforts to retain some semblance of a unified public realm. In the absence of agreement upon what elements can constitute a good in which each and all can share, and in view of the skepticism that many have come to have that there is or can be such a common good, we have settled for a public realm that functions to maintain the one condition we still can deem necessary for any individual's or group's pursuit of what they particularly perceive to be their own good: the maintenance of a maximal range of choice. The most fundamental good, on this account, is simply the power to choose. Under this condition, which the public realm is charged to maintain, the question of the good of what is chosen by any individual or group is not to be raised, either by the polity, or by any other social institution, save under one condition — namely, if one's choice interferes with the choice, or the power to choose, of another. Except for this circumstance, one's perception of good, and one's consequent choice of it, is unassailably private.[21]

This picture of a public realm, constituted to secure conditions for a maximal range of individual choice, is certainly consistent with the view that freedom has its most fundamental exercise in the individual's power to choose. It is, however, a misleading picture inasmuch as it makes impossible of attainment any form of abiding human community. It makes such community impossible of attainment because it is a picture that makes the very bases for such community — the recognition of our human likenesses and the possibility of our going on together — themselves mere matters of choice. This picture leaves out of its understanding of human freedom and, consequently, out of its understanding of the moral dimensions of human choice the human interdependence that is a necessary component of the moral reality of human freedom. What it fails to perceive is the ironic fact that fundamental to the moral reality of human freedom and, consequently, definitive of the moral function of human choice, are items about which we have no choice: our likeness to one another and our need to go on together. These necessities give freedom its moral intelligibility.

Kant recognized these facts in his characterization of the exercise of human moral autonomy as the will of an agent that is determined in accord with one's own, and each other's, membership in a "kingdom of ends." It is of some consequence to note that, for Kant, membership in a kingdom of ends is not something we choose; it is something we recognize to be a necessary component of human moral reality. It is one form in which we recognize reason's interest in the outcome of our moral conduct for the attainment of good for each and for all in an abiding moral community.[22]

The image of the kingdom of ends, which Kant uses to mark out the recognition of human likeness and interdependence that are essential to freedom, gives one indication of the "world-constructing" character that, as noted earlier, gives form to reason's interest. To complete the case made in this chapter for the ordering of freedom to mutuality, I shall show this concern for totality and interconnectedness, which is a mark of reason's interest, to be that which requires human freedom to shape our conduct to the service of human mutuality: reason's interest, when it takes the guise of what Kant calls "moral faith," makes manifest that our freedom is ordered to mutuality. Moral faith makes manifest that our freedom is ordered to mutuality because it is the form in which reason's interest requires that we acknowledge the finitude of our human conduct.[23] This acknowledgment has its origin in what I noted earlier as the particular focus of reason's interest in the exercise of freedom: the efficacy of our moral conduct. Reason's interest takes this focus because, in Kant's view, the sureness we have of our freedom brings no corresponding sureness about that which will result from conduct governed by our freedom. Kant speaks of this concern in terms of the due apportionment of happiness to virtue.[24] To take this concern as a form of reason's interest — which is what Kant does in his account of moral faith — has important consequences for the scope of our representation of such an apportionment — that is, for our picture of human destiny, and the function of our freedom within that picture.

Human Destiny: Happiness and Moral Personality

Kant's concern for the due apportionment of happiness to virtue has far too frequently been caricatured as a narrow philosophical interpretation of Christian beliefs about an individual's eternal reward or punishment. This caricature forgets three elements of Kant's concern, each of which plays a role in his depiction of moral faith. These elements show his concern to be more sweeping in scope and more challenging in content than any doctrine of individual reward and punishment. These elements also reinforce the view that Kant conceives of human freedom, exercised for the attainment of this destiny, to be ordered to the service of human mutuality.

The first element that is often overlooked is the ordering of human cravings and desires to the attainment of happiness. Kant never doubts that we each have a fundamental desire for happiness, and that our particular desires are each expressions of this fundamental human craving. He also never doubts that this craving for happiness is one that our conduct must duly acknowledge.[25]

The second element, which is overlooked even more frequently, is that Kant affirms happiness to be a component of human moral personality. This may strike us as odd in view of the usual identification Kant's commentators make of moral personhood and autonomy, conceived as an individual's power of choice. Yet Kant has good reason to consider it to be such a component: although the attainment of happiness is set to us as a fundamen-

tal human task, its attainment seems to escape our grasp in the
fundamental human endeavor of the exercise of freedom. Thus
the attainment of happiness is a limiting condition to the moral
significance of autonomy and to what we are critically justified
in expecting of it. As such a limit, attainment of happiness can
be considered to function as an essential component of moral personhood. Autonomy, if it is properly exercised, does not bring
about that attainment; it simply secures a condition for such attainment: worthiness for it.[26] In and of itself, autonomy does
not secure happiness for us. A moral personhood that consisted
only in the exercise of autonomy would be for Kant an admira-
ble one, according to the measure with which he admires the
Stoics. It would, nonetheless, be a truncated one, for it would
lack its proper completion: the attainment of happiness.[27]

The third overlooked element is the totality of interconnected
human moral existence into which reason's moral interest requires
that we each place our moral personhood. This means that I cannot represent the completion of my moral personhood in happiness, duly measured to virtue, in an adequate way if I fail to
represent it in a full connection with the completion of moral
personhood for each and every one whom I can acknowledge
as "like me." I must, in other words, be able to represent the
satisfaction of my human desire for happiness in such a way that
it is not for me alone, but also for each and every other person
whom I acknowledge to share in the human communality of
freedom.

Moral Faith: The Expectations of Finite Reason

Each of these elements functions to mark out aspects of the
human finitude that is proper to the exercise of what Kant terms
"pure reason, practical in itself" — that is, freedom. This is in keeping with Kant's overall philosophical enterprise, for which the
finitude of reason is made manifest for its theoretical and practical uses in the guise of "givenness." For the theoretical use of
reason, there is the givenness of sense; for the practical use of
reason in shaping human conduct, there is the givenness of freedom as a "fact"; for the use of reason in which its theoretical
and practical interests join — that is, for the hope, which the exercise of our reason offers us, that the outcome of our conduct

will be abiding good — there is the givenness of the structure of human craving as it is ordered to the attainment of happiness.[28]

I take Kant's doctrine of moral faith to be an account of the way we are enabled to focus our hope in accord with the givenness of our finitude. Kant offers his account of moral faith so that we can acknowledge this finitude in the shape we give to our most fundamental and all-encompassing human expectations — that is, for the attainment of our human destiny. Reason gives shape to these expectations by representing, in terms of totality and interconnectedness, the ordering of human cravings to the attainment of happiness. These expectations are, thereby, concerned with human destiny. Reason's interest requires that they be representations of the good outcome, not just of my own conduct, but of the totality of human conduct.

Kant takes his critical principles to show that human reason is finite. It therefore cannot give these expectations just any shape that makes them accord with its "interest" in totality and interconnectedness. It can give them just the shape of totality and interconnectedness that recognizes the limits that reason must impose on itself in view of the givenness of sense, of freedom, and of the ordering of human craving to the attainment of happiness. Kant, as a result, acknowledges just three ways for reason to represent expectations that accord with these limits. They are the highest good, God, and immortality. He terms these three the "things of faith."[29]

Each of the items that Kant terms a thing of faith represents an aspect of the expectation for the good outcome of human conduct that we can have in accord with the limits reason must place on itself. The chief limit reason places upon the representation of our expectations is the acknowledgment of the likeness to another that I have termed the finitude of our human conduct. The things of faith thereby function to delimit the moral future we can expect from the exercise of freedom — that is, from shaping our conduct to the service of mutuality — even while acknowledging the finitude of that freedom — that is, that it is not fully within the power of this particular item of conduct, or any particular item of conduct, or any combination of these items, to effect the abiding completion of mutuality in the full attainment of human community. Each of these items functions to remind us of an essential characteristic of conduct shaped by human freedom, which manifests the ordering of that freedom to the service of mutuality: such conduct involves entrusting it to others, both in the present and for the future, for a more complete reading of its significance, for recognizing it as a manifestation of our identity in freedom with one another, and for bringing forth from it the fulness of its power for attaining human community.

Kant's account of moral faith, as I have interpreted it, can be taken to be a presentation of the implications of a twofold acknowledgment that lies at the core of Kant's rendering of human moral experience. One acknowledgment is of the ordering of freedom to the service of mutuality; the other is of the finitude of our moral conduct for the abiding attainment of good. Kant's doctrine of moral faith marks out, in the guise of the objects that serve as the "things of faith," the points at which these acknowledgments intersect. It is of particular importance for the claim presented in the next chapter — about the power by which moral autonomy can render us open to an acknowledgment of God's transcendence — that we take clear note of how the doctrine of moral faith allows us to mark out such points of intersection: it does so in virtue of making the future serve as the perspective from which to take sight of human moral existence as it can be shaped to satisfy reason's interest.

The effort I have made to highlight features of Kant's account of moral faith will prove useful for my argument about the role of freedom at the foundation of moral theology if it succeeds in making just this single point: the future provides the perspective from which we can catch clearest sight of the essential ordering of freedom to the service of human mutuality. I do not think it accidental that interpretations of Kant that take his account of freedom to be an effort to understand the individual's power of choice find his doctrines of hope and moral faith a bit perplexing. They frequently resolve the perplexity either by taking them to be anomalous residues of the Christian beliefs in God and eternal salvation, or by trying to turn them into a charter for secularism and for humanity on its own. Neither move does justice to the coherence and comprehensiveness of Kant's thought. Neither proves helpful for resolving the tension between the power of choice and the demands of freedom that are consequent upon the acknowledgment of mutuality and the finitude of our conduct as the frame that reason provides us for disciplining our efforts to fashion a moral world.

Kant's doctrine of moral faith provides us with a perspective of the future from which we can take a fresh look at his understanding of freedom. In it he envisions a future in which the world has been given an abiding shape by human conduct. This world bears the mark of reason: it can be fully shared by each and by all. This world bears the mark of reason because the human conduct that gives it this abiding shape has been governed by reason in its "practical" guise: freedom. This makes it plain that, from the perspective of the future, Kant understands freedom to be essentially ordered to mutuality; its primary function is to govern our conduct toward the shaping of a fully shared world.

Freedom's Venture into Mutuality:
Moral Theology at its Foundations

Showing that Kant understands freedom to be ordered to the service of mutuality does not, of course, require us to understand freedom in the same way. Kant might well be mistaken. The case for understanding freedom in this way cannot rest primarily upon the authority of a particular philosopher. It must rest, instead, upon the adequacy with which this way of understanding freedom elucidates the forms of our human activity and experience. There is, however, a peculiarity, marking our efforts to understand freedom, that makes the determination of the adequacy of this, or any philosophical account of it, particularly difficult. This is a peculiarity, moreover, that bears upon the relationship between philosophical and theological considerations in the argument I have been setting forth. This peculiarity is that the elucidation that an understanding of freedom gives to the forms of our human activities and experience cannot simply be conceptual; it must also be "practical." It must not only allow us to delimit in a reflective manner the conditions that give our activities and experience their particular forms; it must also make it possible for us to refashion those conditions. For an understanding of freedom to be adequate, therefore, it must be one that both elucidates our human activities and experience and makes it possible for them to be transformed.

This peculiarity has its basis in the source from which our understanding of freedom must arise — that is, the very exercise of freedom. There are many philosophical puzzles that can be generated when we try to give an account of the relationship of our understanding of freedom to its source in the exercise of freedom. Only one need concern us here, the most central one: if our understanding of freedom has its origin in the exercise of freedom, then we cannot fully understand — either conceptually or practically — freedom to be essentially ordered to the service of human mutuality unless we are already exercising it in such service. This puzzle must be of concern to us because it clearly indicates that philosophical efforts to show the ordering of freedom to mutuality will have little possibility of success, save when they are addressed to those who have already placed the exercise of their freedom in service to human mutuality. If I exercise my freedom only according to the paradigm that Western culture has taken to be paramount — the representation of an individual's uncoerced power of choice — I will be unable to see how freedom can be at the service of mutuality. Thus, for a philosophical argument for the ordering of freedom to the service of mutuality to succeed, a prior condition must be met. But this prior condition seems beyond the scope of the conceptual considerations of a philosophical argument to effect. This prior condition is trust: inasmuch as the exercise of freedom in the service of mutuality is a condition of the possibility for understanding the mutuality that freedom serves, we must first venture our freedom into the service of human mutuality. Only then shall we be able to make a conceptual delineation of the forms of mutuality that freedom serves.

We ordinarily do not venture our freedom into the service of mutuality on the basis of philosophical considerations: such venturing looks forward, whereas philosophical considerations look back. Once we have ventured, philosophical considerations help us see whence we have come. This helps to explain the particular genius of Kant's account of hope: in it he gives his philosophical considerations a prospect of the future from which to look back upon the exercise of our freedom. His genius here, it should be noted, is not so much philosophical as imaginative. This suggests one useful way to delimit the scope of the philosophical considerations I have offered in this chapter and, thus, to indicate why my argument must now turn to considerations of a quite different kind.

Philosophical considerations, such as the one Kant offers in his account of hope, can bring us only to the threshold of venturing our freedom. They illumine our experience insofar as they bring it to mind that we have, without being fully cognizant of it, in some way already made ventures into mutuality with our freedom. Philosophical considerations, constructed as they are in terms of large, elusive, and reflective concepts such as freedom, good, and mutuality, can, at best, prod us to look back to what we have already done, or to what we are now doing, to note in those activities the features those concepts represent. Even if these philosophical considerations made it clear to us that we have ventured our freedom into the service of human mutuality, they need not move us to venture it again. To do this, different kinds of considerations are called for. They are the considerations that imagination, which can direct our representations of freedom, mutuality, and good toward the future, is best suited to supply.

The form that imagination can take to provide us with considerations that embolden us to venture our freedom into service of mutuality is quite remarkable. As we shall see in the next chapter, imagination takes that form by becoming for us a route of access to what is most fundamentally real. It takes form in what I shall term the "freedom of faith," and in that form gives us access to a life of mutuality with the living God. Imagination, as the freedom of faith, makes moral theology possible as a quest for understanding: it puts us in the presence of God's reality in a way that enables us to understand the moral character of human conduct. It makes it possible for us to see that our conduct can be what we could neither make nor even think it to be by our own power and wit: sign, instrument, and presence of God's own life. Imagination makes it possible for us to see the most basic function of freedom at the foundation of moral theology: God's mutuality enabling our mutuality.

4. Image and Gift:
The Practice of Freedom as
the Foundation of Moral Theology

I. HUMAN DESTINY: EXPECTATION AND PROMISE

Mutuality: God's Venture

The exercise of our freedom is a venture into the moral future.
I have made use of Kant's account of the origin of hope in freedom
to argue that this venture discloses the character of the moral
future: the completion of human mutuality in the full attainment of human community. I then proceeded to claim that, if
the moral future disclosed in the exercise of human freedom is
this full attainment of human community, freedom is itself ordered to the service of human mutuality. The task of this chapter
is to complete the account of how freedom, so ordered to the
service of mutuality, provides the appropriate foundation for the
quest of moral theology for understanding.

The account of the role of freedom at the foundation of moral
theology will be completed by showing it to be that venture into
the moral future that discloses the fundamental reality and truth
of the moral world: that world is constituted by God's venture
to invite us to share in the inner mutuality of divine life. The
moral world can be shown to have this fundamental reality and
truth — that it is God's venture, not just our own — insofar as the
exercise of our freedom is allowed to make manifest that the
ground of its ordering to mutuality is God's mutuality, freely
shared. Disclosure of the moral world as God's venture makes

108

it plain as well why we must represent that reality as pledge and promise for the sake of shaping conduct. God's venture respects, even while transforming, those ways in which human freedom, even when exercised without explicit awareness of God's venture, gives us access to the reality of the completion of human mutuality in human community. Because those ways — the exercise of moral imagination, which discloses to us the promise of community in our human likenesses, and the conduct shaped by such imagination, which fulfills that promise in practices fostering ever more inclusive mutuality — take their focus on the moral future, they require that we represent the world to which they give us access as a world of what ought to be.

In consequence of the constitution of the moral world as God's venture, human freedom and imagination can take form as effective signs — that is, sacraments — of God's mutuality, enabling human mutuality to attain its completion in the fulness of human community. This "sacramental" form should, therefore, be the mark of the exercise of freedom in Christian life: under the guidance of imagination freedom shapes our conduct into practices that are to make present to the world the reality of the abiding attainment of human community that has been enabled by the gift of God's mutuality. In the next chapter, I shall describe some of the contexts of contemporary life that stand in particular need of conduct shaped into the practices that make present a mutuality that enables the attainment of human community. In this chapter, I shall show that the practices that make present such mutuality are those which, shaped by the exercise of a human freedom, thereby acknowledge the reality of the moral world by their responsiveness to the venture of God's mutuality.

Hope and the Practice of Freedom

We represent the moral future in correlation with our understanding of freedom. In the preceding chapter, I noted how freedom, understood in terms of mutuality, finitude, and its world-constructing character, enables us to fashion our representation of the moral future in a particular way: as the human community in virtue of which there is to be the satisfaction of human cravings. This is not the only way it has been possible to understand the correlation of freedom with the moral future. When freedom is understood as the exercise of the individual's power to choose, it provides a model for understanding human freedom that neither requires nor enables us to represent the moral future in terms of community. It requires us, instead, to represent the moral future in terms of a destiny in which each of us stands apart from one another.

This way of understanding freedom thus neither requires nor enables freedom to serve as the ground for hope in the attainment of community, and so precludes it from serving as the foundation for the quest of moral theology for understanding. This is so because it severs freedom from the mutuality that engenders our hope for human community, and stands as the first invitation to venture our freedom along the path on which God invites us to share in the mutuality that is his own life. This severance of freedom from mutuality can be questioned not only because it makes it impossible for freedom to serve as the foundation for moral theology; it also can be questioned because, as we shall see shortly, it allows us to give conduct a shape that renders unintelligible not only our hope for human community, but the very exercise of human freedom as well.[1]

Kant's account of freedom steers us clear of such difficulties in its rendering of the relationship this hope bears to freedom. It shows how the quest of moral theology is possible by noting clearly what can and what cannot be affirmed about this hope once philosophical considerations reach their limits. It thus affirms that the completion of our moral action lies in the future and that its term is in a good shareable in virtue of one's membership in an abiding community. Yet in view of the manifest finitude of our conduct in its effecting of good, this account remains silent in regard to the manner in which that highest good at last will come to be. It thus affirms as well that even though all human moral endeavor must be ordered to that completion, and is necessary for its coming to be, it is, nonetheless, not sufficient. Such sufficiency is given in virtue of God's moral ordering of the totality of human freedom engaged in moral endeavor. This account, however, remains silent in regard to the manner in which God works concretely to bring about such ordering.

We may summarize the limits that Kant's account places on the philosophical articulation of human hope for the moral future in these terms: in accord with philosophical considerations we can represent the human destiny of moral community in virtue of which there is the satisfaction of human cravings as an expectation well founded upon the exercise of human freedom. Those considerations, however, are not sufficient to enable us to acknowledge it according to its most fundamental reality: as the outcome of a promise of mutuality freely given by a transcendent God.[2]

The former way of representing human destiny is congruent with and preparatory of the latter, but it is not equivalent to it. There is a hope in human destiny that is founded upon human freedom exercised in moral endeavor. Philosophy has as one of its tasks the articulation of the freedom that gives rise to this hope and the consequences that this hope and its foundation in freedom have for understanding and shaping our conduct. There is a hope in human destiny that is founded upon the freedom of faith that responds to the revelation of God's promise. Moral theology has as one of its tasks the articulation of the freedom of faith that gives rise to this hope and its relationship to the freedom of moral endeavor. In the light of what is thereby articulated, moral theology then has the task of specifying the consequences that this hope, and its foundation in a freedom that has its exercise both in moral endeavor and in faith, have for understanding and shaping our conduct.

The grounds that make it necessary for philosophy to fall silent in articulating human hope for the moral future are ones Kant would term "practical": they are fundamental to the proper exercise of freedom. This silence, however, does not mark the end of human concern with the hope that philosophy's account of human freedom can and does affirm. In offering Kant's account as the basis for understanding the role of freedom as the foundation for moral theology, I am proposing something he did not: I am proposing that this concern can continue as a quest for understanding even after philosophy falls silent. Such a quest is possible as long as it continues to be undertaken "critically," in Kant's sense of that term: it marks out and respects the limits of human reason. Moral theology, as the continuation of this quest, can therefore be "critical" inasmuch as it both functions and has its origin within the limits that the exercise of freedom (i.e., reason in its moral use) requires us to respect. In particular, the quest of moral theology for understanding can be undertaken critically inasmuch as it functions and has its origin within the limits that freedom manifests to us as marks of finitude. These limits are ones philosophical considerations allow us to represent as the hope of the full attainment of human community. Moral theology accepts this limit at the origin of its own quest, yet, by placing this limit within the ambit of faith, it understands it to function in a way philosophy could not articulate: as a sign of God's mutuality.

Kant's account of freedom provides a basis for understanding the role of freedom at the foundation of moral theology because it sees that the expectations we foster for the moral future have their origin in the mutuality to which freedom is ordered. As a result, this provides us with the possibility that such expectations can also be anticipatory of a promise of a mutuality that, when accepted, shows itself to be a reality that exceeds our hopes, and is their ground as well. Kant's account of freedom thus provides a way for us to construct a foundation for moral theology in an age for which philosophical renderings of human freedom that place it in service of human mutuality seem unavailable and, even when available, often are taken by philosophers and theologians alike to be curious relics of a more metaphysically inclined age.[3]

Kant's account of human freedom is one that many have thought it best to cut down to more modest size. His talk of freedom as the point that gives us entry and membership in a realm of the "noumenal" or "supersensible" is thereby explained away, presumably without detriment to the central features of his doctrine of moral autonomy.[4] Once it is cut down to size, however, freedom loses its power to serve as ground for hope in the full attainment of human community. Kant's talk of the supersensible functions as a reference point for raising the question of human moral destiny, because that talk marks out the inherent mutuality of freedom. It is thereby also a reference point for the hope, grounded in freedom, that Kant takes to provide the appropriate response to this question. Without this reference point, the doctrine of hope, with its focus upon the destiny of each and all, represented as the "highest good," becomes idle. Freedom conceived without inherent mutuality need not concern itself with human moral destiny; it need only be preoccupied with its own integrity.

A philosophical analysis of human freedom that has the power to uncover its inherent mutuality also has the power to show how freedom is foundational for moral theology. This is so because the mutuality to which freedom is ordered is fundamental for representing, both as expectation and as promise, a communion of persons as the destined final outcome of human moral conduct. This philosophical analysis is foundational but it is not itself moral theology: the expectation that the full attainment of human community will be our moral destiny — which is the hope engendered by the mutuality of freedom — is different from the promise that it will be. All that philosophy can do — and doing it constitutes its foundational task — is leave the expectation open to the promise. That it does leave it so open, moreover, can best be seen retrospectively, from the vantage point of the moral theology whose quest it thereby founds.

Human Conduct and the Disclosure of Mutuality

However complete and adequate a philosophical analysis of human freedom may be, it will prove insufficient for use at the foundation of moral theology if, as seems to be the case in our contemporary culture, we shape our lives in accord with practices that all too often conceal, rather than reveal, the inherent ordering of freedom to mutuality. Such practices do not provide a basis on which to form expectations of a shared human destiny. Even less do they anticipate the manner in which such expectations will be met: as gift. These practices, instead, leave us with little expectation of a personal, let alone a shared, moral destiny as the outcome of our conduct. All too often the most our contemporary understandings of freedom allow us to expect from its exercise are moments of individual self-satisfaction.

If much of our contemporary intellectual and cultural practice leaves us with little reason, and even less incentive, to form expectations of human moral destiny, then showing the ordering of freedom to mutuality to be a foundation for moral theology is more than just a conceptual exercise. It is an initial step in an effort to refashion and, where possible, recover those patterns of human interaction and conduct that disclose the mutuality of freedom, and thereby make possible the expectations of human destiny. From the perspective of many contemporary renditions of human freedom, such patterns of human interaction and conduct, which disclose the ordering of freedom to mutuality, will, no doubt, confront us with a curious duality. These patterns can, on the one hand, make it manifest that shared understanding and mutual trust are the basis for all that we deem certain. Yet patterns of conduct that disclose the mutuality of freedom can be, on the other hand, the ones that appear most fraught with risk and uncertainty prior to our participation in them. These are the patterns of interaction and conduct that call upon the exercise of human freedom in its most radical form: to be enabling and instancing of shared understanding and mutual trust.

The patterns of conduct that disclose, with such curious duality, the mutuality of freedom are those human practices and institutions that instance and express human interdependence in its various forms and human mutual commitment at various levels: friendship and family; scientific inquiry and public worship; neighborhood and polity. The list of such practices and institutions could go on and on; it includes all those whose intelligibility and vitality can be grounded upon the interdependence that is the most radical form of human freedom. As long as they provide an environing form of life, we are not often aware of their rootedness in the mutuality of freedom. When they are subject to question — as most of them have been in recent history — the radical test to which they put freedom becomes clear and, to many, unsettling. It becomes particularly unsettling if our understanding of the mutuality of freedom has been obscured or lost because these institutions and practices have lost contact with their own rootedness in it.[5]

Moral Theology and the Recovery of Mutuality

Moral theology as a reflective enterprise is in a particularly precarious position when the institutions and practices of an age lose their rootedness in the mutuality of freedom. These practices undermine it at its foundation: conduct ceases to take shape in terms of mutuality, and, thereby, to foster and sustain expectations of a shared human moral destiny. In the absence of such expectations, it is far more difficult for us to be rendered open to reception of the promise that such a destiny of mutuality will be accomplished. Though moral theology is placed in a precarious

position under these circumstances, Christian moral life need not
be. Fortunately, the promise does not wait upon the expectation. In fact, the power of the promise is made most manifest
when it is given, even though expectations have ceased. Its power
is such that it can even bring us to recover that mutuality of human freedom from which we have cast ourselves away.

The promise of a communion of persons as our human moral
destiny is disclosed, according to Christian beliefs, by the concrete presence of God's own mutuality through Jesus Christ. In
accord with those same beliefs, such a promise is taken to have
power to make practices of Christian life disclose the mutuality
of freedom. In an age in which central human institutions and
practices lose their rootedness in the mutuality of freedom, practices of Christian life, therefore, can and must serve as prophetic
reminders and calls back to the acknowledgment of human mutuality. The foundational relationship between freedom and
moral theology must first be turned on its head so that it can
later be put right: the promise must guide us to a recovery of
the expectation, so that the expectations of the next age will be
able to recognize the promise more readily. This is true not just
for moral foundations: there are many forms of contemporary
human activity for which what is Christian can begin to serve
as a clue for the recovery of what is human and humanizing,
so that in a later age what is Christian may be acknowledged
as completion of all that is human and humanizing.

II. HUMAN CRAVINGS: THE GIFT OF MUTUALITY

Hope: The Recognition of Cravings as Gift

My argument has focused on hope as a central element in the
foundation that freedom provides for moral theology. The hope
engendered by freedom shapes our expectation of the moral future. It is foundational for the enterprise of moral theology insofar as this expectation can render us open to the reception of that
moral future as promise — as the gracious offering of a transcendent God. In this section I shall propose one way in which we
can be rendered open to receive the moral future as promise:
by understanding that our human cravings have the inherent

character of "gift." If we put into practice expectations that the moral future is to be the abiding completion of human mutuality, we shall be able to see our human cravings as elements that bear the promise of the moral future: we shall be able to see them as gifts ordered to the enablement and exhibition of the mutuality of human freedom. Hope, by enabling us to see our cravings as gifts to be placed in service of mutuality, can thereby serve as a basis from which we can be led to see the moral world in one aspect of its fundamental reality as God's venture. That venture bids us to place in service to an abiding and shared moral future our cravings — those elements of our human reality that, more than anything else, bear the mark of the immediacy and the dividedness of our finitude.

To speak of human cravings as "gifts" is not intended to deny their possession of other characteristics that obscure or even overwhelm this particular character: their importunity upon our putatively rational deliberations; the transitory and often fragmentary character of their satisfaction; their multiple presence, requiring that ordering and choice be made among the objects of their satisfaction. We can obscure the character of human cravings as "gift" in much the same fashion as we obscure the character of freedom as mutuality: by patterns of action formed in virtue of a partial apprehension of their function for the attainment of human destiny. Such partial apprehension and its consequences are often most manifest in those patterns of conduct that, though formed out of a craving for human mutuality, allow only for its partial achievement in scope, expectation, or endurance. Such patterns of conduct deny the hope to which the exercise of freedom gives rise. Among such patterns are those of domination and subservience, which persist as a root form of evil across a whole range of human interaction. Among them, too, are patterns of self-sufficiency and of isolative conduct, which also manifest the form of evil that can take root in partial apprehension of mutuality: despair of fulfillment of the craving for mutuality.

The route that leads from our initial recognition of likeness, as a sign of the mutuality to which our freedom is ordered, to the acknowledgment, in our conduct, that our cravings have a gifted character that enables them to serve that mutuality is a long one. In fact, for most of us it is a route along which we spend a lifetime of travel. Our initial entry upon this route does not take place with full reflection; before we know where such a route leads we begin our initiation and training in those patterns and practices of human interaction that place us in one another's presence as centers of action and of value. Participation in these patterns and practices is a precondition for the recognition of the mutuality of human freedom and, consequently, for awareness of our membership in a moral world. It is a precondition, however, that can guarantee neither the occurrence of the recognition of mutuality, nor its recognition in a way sufficient to bring full awareness of one's membership in a moral world.[6]

Freedom and the Practices of Mutuality

In order to recognize that our freedom is ordered to the service of mutuality, we must be participants in human patterns of mutuality. We can participate in human patterns of mutuality, nonetheless, without thereby either recognizing fully freedom's ordering to mutuality, or placing the exercise of our freedom at the service of mutuality. This creates a set of circumstances that we may find to pose an insoluable dilemma for conduct: we seem called upon to engage in practices whose significance, prior to our engagement in them, we cannot fully grasp and, even after our engagement, may still elude our comprehension. The reasonable course of action in such circumstances would seem to be to refuse to engage in such practices. The ground for such a refusal is that such circumstances do not provide the knowledge requisite for making reasonable a choice to engage in such practices. On the other hand, refusal to engage in at least some of the practices — for instance, friendship — seems unreasonable: some set of such practices seems to constitute the fabric of human social existence.

The reflection I ask students to make upon their experience of friendship provides them with an opportunity to see that, although there is a point to this dilemma, it is nonetheless misleading. In friendship they are already engaged in a practice that calls upon them to put their freedom at the service of mutuality, but it is an engagement that does not arise as merely, or principally, the kind of choice the dilemma presents. They can make friendship an example of such a dilemma only to the extent that they take it to be something their experience indicates it is not: a matter that requires full comprehension before one can be justified in taking it upon oneself. These reflections can also lead them to see that, even though the dilemma arises from a mistake about the fundamental character of freedom, the feature of human moral life on which it takes focus is most central. In dealing with this dilemma we are reminded that the adequacy of our moral understanding rests upon the manner in which we have engaged our freedom. This feature of human moral existence does, in fact, present a difficulty for efforts to show, and efforts to live, the ordering of freedom to mutuality that is far more fundamental than the dilemma for action we have just considered: even engagement in the practices of mutuality does not abolish the possibility that we can deflect the exercise of our freedom in those practices away from the service of mutuality.

This difficulty appears to undercut what my argument has proposed as a fundamental truth of the moral world: the essential ordering of freedom to mutuality. This difficulty makes it plain that freedom can be withdrawn from the service of mutuality. The difficulty is a powerful one to the extent that we take our recognition of the ordering of freedom to mutuality, let alone our living in accord with this ordering, to have its most fundamental source in our own efforts. We will have this understanding to the extent that we fail to see how thoroughgoing is the finitude that our conduct manifests as characteristic of our human freedom. That finitude characterizes even the sureness of our recognition of the ordering of freedom to mutuality; neither the recognition nor the sureness with which we hold it can enduringly stand as products solely of unaided human effort.

We cannot come to full recognition of human likeness and sustain it all by ourselves; it is a recognition that, even in its initial moments, gives sign of being "gift": we find ourselves in the presence of a power over against ourselves, which draws the centering of our world, and the actions we do from such centering, away from ourselves as its main focus. The presence of such a power is often unasked for, and may come in a welcome guise, such as friendship, joy, or love, or in an unwelcome guise, such as disappointment, failure, or suffering. It is not enough for the presence of such a power to turn the main focus of the world away from ourselves if it is both to effect and to sustain recognition of the mutuality of freedom. The focus to which it draws us must also make it possible for us to see, or to see better, that our likeness to one another requires that we place trust in one another to exercise our freedom to form bonds with one another.

These bonds of interdependence, consequent upon our granting trust to one another, mark how this recognition and the gifting that is its source, constitute what is most fundamentally "personal" in human existence. In consequence, the power that shifts the focus of our world to these bonds of interdependence, no matter what the particular occasion of its exercise, can be properly characterized as "personal"; it serves to effect our acknowledgment of one another in the character that constitutes us as persons: the trust that bonds us in fundamental interdependence upon each other.[7]

We thus recognize and sustain our fundamental interdependence in virtue of the hope that has its origin in the acknowledgment of our likeness in the finitude of human conduct. Hope from such a source can recognize mutuality as both goal and gift for the exercise of human freedom. Hope recognizes mutuality as goal by arousing in us the expectation that we can go on together; hope recognizes mutuality as gift by enabling us to entrust to one another the fulfillment of that expectation, both now and in the moral future. Hope allows us to sustain our acknowledgment of likeness in the finitude of human conduct, moreover, as long as our action shows confidence that the goal is dependent upon the gift.

Mutuality and the Shape of Human Destiny

We find it difficult to act with the confidence that the goal is dependent upon the gift. To do so, we have to shape our conduct in accord with the expectation that all forms of human interaction and endeavor will exhibit and foster the shared understanding and mutual trust that enable us to go on together. We have, in fact, quite different expectations about the various forms of human interaction and endeavor. We expect them to foster, first of all, the particular interests of those who interact. We have come to see, for instance, how competition arising from personal pride or ambition, concern for national interests, or hope of eventual market impact can exert strong pressure upon the direction to be taken even by those practices we would hold up as a paradigm of shared understanding and mutual trust: scientific research and inquiry. These pressures deflect the mutual understanding and shared trust that is the precondition for such research and inquiry onto paths from which sight of the mutuality of human freedom — which makes the mutual understanding and shared trust possible — can be lost. We have come to see, for another instance, how half-believed cultural myths, experienced distrust, or deeply rooted anxieties can prevent a parent, confronted with a child's question about death or about sex, from reaching an important moment of shared understanding and mutual trust. These instances suggest, moreover, that human cravings of various kinds — for example, for esteem, control, gratification — themselves often block the way to achievement of a human craving for shared understanding and mutual trust.

Confidence in the power of our conduct to exhibit the shared understanding and trust that serve mutuality is made difficult when cravings are understood, as they seem to be in the shaping moral picture of our culture, as principally instrumental for the attainment of individual good. This picture has dominated European and American moral self-understanding for at least two centuries. It is, of course, the background on which the image of the individual's autonomy is displayed. This picture explains why it is that shared understanding and mutual trust have failed to become effective paradigms for the shaping of human conduct, be it in interpersonal or institutional contexts. This picture does allow us to represent freedom at the foundation of human moral life; yet it is a freedom whose connection to mutuality is one of circumstance. In consequence the human destiny that emerges from such a foundation need not be, and — to the extent to which freedom is seen as ordered solely to serve the good of the individual who exercises it — even cannot be, one of mutuality. We are thus left with a profoundly ambiguous and, in my judgment, ultimately incoherent view of the object of our hope for the outcome of our moral conduct.

This picture of human moral destiny and the foundation of human moral life is portrayed in its richest and most complex form in the tradition of the "social contract." According to this picture, mutuality, though present at the foundation of human moral life and giving form to human destiny, does not have its basis in the inherent character of human freedom. It has its basis, instead, in the exigencies of human cravings, many of which cannot be satisfied save in the context of going on together.

This picture thus provides us with a way of placing human cravings into a picture of human moral destiny. Within that picture, human moral destiny is the maximum attainment of the good for each; this constitutes the sum and the substance of the good for all. In relation to this picture of human moral destiny, our cravings are principally instrumental for the attainment of individual good. As a member of the set of human cravings, a craving for mutuality—for abiding patterns of shared understanding and mutual trust—enjoys no special status by which it is to be valued and fostered by each and by all. It may be included as one element in the subset of human cravings—for example, survival, esteem—that appear common to us all. In that case its value for each and all lies in the fact of its apparent universality, not in its specific character as a craving for shared understanding and mutual trust. If, moreover, it is not even included within the subset of cravings that have a claim to universality, then its value for any one of us will have an even more precarious status. Its value will lie merely in whatever instrumentality it has for helping us satisfy the full range of our cravings.[8]

In this picture of a moral world, moral principles are understood as the best we can do to maintain a social form for moral conduct in the face of the pressure of the interests expressed by and in our cravings. These principles can give us no more, however, than the assurance that we are to be accorded a fair opportunity to satisfy at least those cravings common to all, and that the satisfaction of cravings peculiar to some should not interfere with that fair opportunity. In such a picture, shared understanding and mutual trust take on value insofar as they can be shown to be necessary and effective means to the establishment and maintenance of fair opportunity to satisfy at least those cravings common to all.

This picture of a moral world does not provide us with resources adequate for representing human destiny according to a form by which it is inherently shared: it conceives of the sharing of interests and cravings as taking place principally in their pursuit, not in their attainment. Although it might allow us to stretch imagination to the point of conceiving of the satisfaction of human craving as a "gift," it cannot let us so conceive of the craving itself. It must remain exigency, not gift.

Freedom: Craving as the Gift of Finitude

As long as we think of our cravings as exigencies, the principal function of freedom with respect to them can be conceived only as the exercise of the power of choice. We exercise our freedom by choosing which of these cravings to satisfy and the appropriate means to their satisfaction. Our cravings are ordered to freedom as objects for the exercise of its choice; freedom serves our cravings by shaping conduct to their satisfaction.

We can think otherwise of our cravings; we can think of them as gifts. We can think of them this way, however, only if we venture to exercise our freedom to shape our conduct in service of human mutuality. In that venture, our cravings can be ordered, like freedom, to human mutuality in view of the hope we have for an abiding achievement of human community. When so ordered, our cravings can be understood not as exigencies, but as gifts: they are capable of being ventured to foster shared understanding and mutual trust. This capability is not an exigency; our cravings do not importune us to be placed in the service of mutuality. Instead, in the context of this venture of freedom, they are presented to us as an invitation, an opportunity that they also be fashioned to accord with that which makes us fully human: the acknowledgment of our likeness to, and our interdependence upon, one another, whose sign is the finitude of our conduct. Our venturing to foster these constitutive elements of human mutuality, moreover, shows freedom to be itself craving and, in consequence, gift. It is the craving that is the most fundamental gift of our finitude: to share of ourselves so that we can be complete in and for one another.

The imaginative stretching that allows us to think of our cravings as "gifts" takes place, therefore, when in our conduct we accord to the ordering of freedom to mutuality — made manifest as the craving for shared understanding and mutual trust — a unifying and central role for the whole set of human cravings. In this unifying role we may speak of it as a rational craving. As such, it functions as moral governor and touchstone for the direction and the assessment of all human cravings.[9]

The craving for shared understanding and mutual trust thus has a dual character that makes it the central hinge upon which to fasten the final elements of my argument to show the role of freedom at the foundation of moral theology. These elements will show that the acknowledgment, made in our conduct, of the ordering of freedom to mutuality renders us open to the acknowledgment that the moral world is constituted by God's venture of inviting us to share in the life of his mutuality. The dual character this craving manifests is that of rationality and gift. In its root and foundation, this craving is rational—that is, marked with the world-constructing character that Kant has set forth as proper to the rationality of human freedom. In its effective presence for shaping our conduct, however, this craving comes as "gift": the reliable promise of the full attainment of moral community. As "gift" it allows us to shape our conduct even now in accord with that attainment, in anticipation of its abiding presence, which can come only later.

This craving provides us with a focus from which to take sight of the fundamental constitution of the moral world. When we act in accord with this craving, we acknowledge the reality of that world to be in its ordering to the abiding attainment of mutuality. Although this acknowledgment takes place first and foremost in conduct, it has a reflective side to it, which can be posed in the concepts of philosophy: we reflectively acknowledge the reality of the moral world by marking out the rational character of human freedom to be constituted in and by our craving for shared understanding and mutual trust. This craving and the exercise of our freedom in accord with it, are both manifestations of reason's interest that our conduct be world-constructing. The world that reason guides us to represent in accord with the exercise of our freedom, moreover, is the one that accords also with the acknowledgment of the finitude of our conduct: a world fashioned in hope of the abiding achievement of human mutuality, yet marked by the recognition that its attainment still lies beyond the power of our conduct.

The concrete mark that the rationality of our freedom should therefore impress upon our conduct is willingness to make the fostering of mutuality its governing principle. Our conduct does not always bear this mark. In fact, we most often find ourselves unwilling so to fashion our conduct. Our unwillingness marks out the limit we seek to impose upon our moral rationality: the power of freedom, simply as rational, to govern our conduct. Our unwillingness, however, need not stand unchallenged as the point of closure for the power of reason to be the engine of our freedom. There is, as counterweight to this unwillingness, the possibility of recognizing and receiving the craving for mutuality in its power as "gift." In this power lies the possibility of a transformation of reason that enables us to overcome our unwillingness. Reason is transformed into the capacity of imagination to be touched concretely by the power of God's transcendence.

Our unwillingness has many grounds. The most pervasive is a sense — often a fear — that governance of our conduct in accord with mutuality requires us to postpone or to minimize the satisfaction of other cravings. Even when we put it in the guise of reason's interest, we can invest our craving for shared understanding and mutual trust with far too little power to overcome such fear. We let it become an abstract concern for representing our conduct as universal, rather than letting it be the power to shape our conduct concretely in accord with the acknowledgment that we are all one in the finitude of our conduct. Even when the abstract concern for representing our conduct as universal is allowed shaping presence for our conduct, there are elements of our own interest to which we almost never fully deny power to direct the interest of reason: we hardly ever forget to calculate the ways in which mutuality can serve to bring about the satisfaction of our other cravings.

Our unwillingness to make the fostering of human mutuality the governing rule for our conduct also manifests itself as a lack of surety: we lack confidence in the power of shared understanding and mutual trust to shape our conduct. Giving trust makes us vulnerable, because the giving of trust can be betrayed. The sharing of understanding can be threatening, because we may someday find cherished beliefs, when put to the test of that shared understanding, proved wanting. Even when we have, in consequence of shared understanding and mutual trust, surety of what we ought to do and of what we can do, that is often still not enough to generate the confidence that leads to the doing of the deed. Thus even when trust is secured and understanding is shared, they lead a precarious existence in the interplay of human interests.

In the face of our unwillingness and our lack of surety, the craving for mutuality can nonetheless become an effective presence for shaping conduct. Reason's interest in constructing a world that is the completion of human mutuality makes it possible for hope to give its form to this craving. When formed by hope, this craving can enter the interplay of human interests as "gift." When recognized as gift, this craving even becomes a surety for the moral future. The concrete forms that hope gives this craving and makes it offer as gift are manifold: they are found in persons, in tales and images, in institutions and practices, in the exemplary and paradigmatic deeds that portray the starts and the sustainings of our goings on together. These forms are also "imaginative," in that imagination is the power to make present to us, in its reality, what should be. Through imagination, these forms call upon us, in virtue of our craving for mutuality, to make present, through our conduct, that which is not yet but which should be: the abiding human community that completes our craving for mutuality.

Recognition that our human freedom takes form as a craving for mutuality and is thus constituted as the fundamental gift of human finitude opens for us a prospect upon a moral world that is quite different from the one represented from the prospect of the social contract. In this world, our pledges to go on together are made not simply in view of their service to a particular range of shared human interests; they are made, first and foremost, as sign and acknowledgment of care for one another as a fundamental mark of the human. From the prospect of this world, such pledges serve as effective sign of our hope in the completion of our craving for mutuality. They are offered in the knowledge that the completion of this craving is beyond our power to effect in full and abiding fashion. They are nonetheless offered with confidence that our conduct, shaped in fidelity to these pledges, can be put at the service of such completion. These pledges entrust our craving for mutuality to one another for the moral future.

In order to recognize freedom as a gift, and as the fundamental gift of human finitude, we must have the imagination to see clearly the context in which it is offered. That context is provided by the two necessities we acknowledge as the very conditions for moral life: that we are like one another and that we must go on together. Though we must go on together, our doing so need not be marked by care for the well-being of each and all, or even of any, who journey with us. In this context, freedom is offered us as a gift for our going on together by enabling us to mark it with such care and to pledge fidelity to such marking. We are already bound to one another by the conditions of our moral life; freedom enables us to take up that bond as a pledge to give faithful care to one another. It is as enabling power for fidelity that freedom manifests its character as gift.[10]

In this power, freedom is yet marked with finitude. Even though, in virtue of our freedom, we can pledge fidelity to care for one another, our freedom lacks the power to redeem that pledge in full. The finitude that freedom manifests here — that in enabling us to pledge fidelity, it shows us the limits of our power to be faithful — is of central importance to its role at the foundation of moral theology. The finitude that freedom manifests here shows that, though the fidelity needed to sustain our going on together must have its source in freedom, our finite and often fragmented freedom cannot claim to be that source. In its power to enable us to pledge fidelity, however, it points to the freedom that is that source: the freedom of God, acknowledged as transcendent, who has first pledged fidelity to us.[11]

Thus our pledge to care for one another's good as we go on together, enabled by freedom, made in full awareness of our powerlessness to be guarantors of its abiding fulfillment, yet made to be faithfully kept, stands as a sign of the most fundamental "gifting" that characterizes freedom. We can recognize this sign in conduct that we give over to be shaped in fidelity to our pledges to care for one another as we go on together, in full awareness of our powerlessness to bring the mutuality we each crave to its lasting completion. For our conduct to be so shaped, resources of mind and heart must be touched at a level that is so fundamental that they can function as one: the level of imagination. In the presence of our human craving for mutuality, given form as hope by the exercise of freedom for its attainment, imagination becomes our human mode of access to the fundamental conditions for mutuality's completion. Narrative provides the basic form in which imagination keeps this access open. Particular tales of human conduct shaped by mutuality or misshaped by its neglect serve as reminders and as partial glimpses of what we hope to be and of the fundamental conditions in which we must sustain our hope: an abiding craving for mutuality, yet a powerlessness to bring about its lasting satisfaction, except in the world that hope empowers us to imagine.

Hope: The Empowerment of Imagination

Here we touch the limits of reason again: it is not given to our reason, nor to our will, nor even to our action, but only to our imagination — the most "idle" of our capabilities — to show us how our craving for mutuality is brought to completion. This is gracious irony: our otherwise powerless imagination effects over and over what all the resources of human will, enterprise, and wit have long fruitlessly struggled to make real. Here too may be the gracious hint of how this reality comes to be: through our powerlessness becoming power, in the form of hope, from one who does effect far beyond what we can ask, or think, or even dream.

Hope empowers imagination to make manifest to us the reality of the moral world in which there is abiding attainment of human community. Hope so empowers imagination in the venture of our freedom to the service of mutuality. We make that venture in the pledges we offer, both explicitly and implicitly, to care for one another's good. Hope empowers imagination to see that the sign and presence of the moral world is the fidelity of our conduct to these pledges. Imagination engenders narrative to make the fidelity of human conduct present to us, because the world of what is far too seldom allows us to see such fidelity of conduct to the pledges of mutuality come to term in the full achievement of human community.

Hope empowers us to represent the moral world in the guise of imagination, not because that world fails to be real, but because our capacity to represent what is real — particularly with respect to the destiny to which we are called in the exercise of our freedom — is limited. It is limited by our finitude, which requires us to represent it as it ought to be. It is limited further by our unwillingness to enter fully through our conduct into the venture of mutuality. This unwillingness causes us to doubt that what we represent as what ought to be has full title to be called "real." Hope makes it possible for us to affirm that this world of what ought to be is real, even in the face of these limitations. Hope does so insofar as it is itself empowered by, and thereby made the instrument of, God's transcendence touching and transforming human lives.

The final turn of my argument, therefore, must direct us to a consideration of hope as the empowering presence of God's transcendence for the exercise of human freedom. This consideration will lead us to see that, as the freedom of human moral endeavor functions to open up for us the possibility to hope in a shared human destiny, it is rendered open to transformation into the freedom of faith. In consequence of this transformation, our quest to understand and to govern human conduct rightly can take form as the enterprise I term moral theology. This is so because this transformation enables us to locate the origin of the craving for mutuality that is the root form of our freedom. Its origin lies in the gift of life offered to us in God's own mutuality, which is continually made present to us as the narrative of God's abiding fidelity to his pledge of mutuality to his people. This narrative is of the abiding presence of God's word, in Scripture, church, and world.

III. HOPE, IMAGINATION, AND TRANSCENDENCE: THE GIFT OF TRUTH

The Limits of Reason and the Credibility of Hope

At the limits of reason, hope allows us to approach a truth of our human reality that gives a fundamental form to our lives. It is a truth we often would rather not recognize. This truth is about our mortality and our finitude: left to our own devices, our cravings go unsatisfied, even as they have so gone for the numberless generations before us.

Yet by venturing us into the service of mutuality, freedom gives rise to a hope that enables us to approach this truth without fear: the satisfaction of our cravings is possible, even in the face of our finitude, provided that we are faithful to the form of our existence that gathers us into moral community. Such hope provides a context in which to understand and to try to live with this truth. Yet it may not convince us to accept this context, because the condition it presents for the satisfaction of our cravings is offered only as pledge, not as accomplishment. If we accept this hope, it can make the realization of the truth of our mortality and finitude poignant and, frequently enough, tragic: because of our mortality and our finitude we fail to keep faithful to the condition for redemption of the pledge. Left to our own devices, our cravings go without satisfaction because we seek satisfaction first, rather than its most fundamental condition: mutual trust. In our zeal for satisfying our cravings we fail to remain faithful to the form of our existence as moral community. We fail most often, perhaps, because we find the hope unpersuasive, if not incredible: to be bound in trust to one another seems not to be the way to get what we crave.[12]

There is truth to this: to be bound in trust to one another is not, and cannot be, a means to the satisfaction of human craving. In virtue of this truth, the very human freedom that has generated hope as the most radical expression of reason's interest runs the risk of now taking its own hope to be illusion. When we take this hope for illusion, however, it is a sign that we have failed to make reason's interest fully our own, in that form it takes when we approach the limits set by our finitude. That form is imagination. In virtue of imagination, we can represent being bound in trust to one another as a fundamental condition for the satisfaction of human craving without thereby representing it as a means. We can represent it as itself the satisfaction of our most fundamental human craving, without which the satisfaction of other cravings, no matter how full, no matter how varied, fails to make sense.

The hope to which freedom gives rise allows us to approach the unsettling truth of our mortality and finitude. It invites us to acknowledge this truth in a context that enables us to shape our conduct, mortal and finite though it may be, to remain faithful to our pledges of mutuality. Freedom, as an exercise of reason's interest, gives rise to this hope; yet we often, in the name of reason, mistrust this hope. We do so because the bonds of mutual trust and shared understanding that are conditions for the attainment of this hope seem impossible to fulfill because of the imperious character of our multiple human cravings. Reason here formulates its sardonic version of a gospel dictum: seek first all the other things you crave; the kingdom of ends may be given you besides—but do not count on it.

Transformation of Reason: The Narrative Context

We can do no better than this unless we allow our reason to be transformed into the power that allows us to be touched by the reality of the world that hope represents as pledge. That power is imagination. This transformation of reason into imagination can take place in consequence of our attentive listening to and recounting of narrative. In narrative, we are brought to encounter our mortality and finitude transformed to the service of mutuality in view of the completion that hope pledges.[13] In narrative, we can represent the concrete ways in which bonds of mutual trust and shared understanding must stand and be sustained, in virtue of our mortality and finitude, as the fundamental conditions for the moral intelligibility of our cravings and their satisfaction. Narrative, however strange its content, however detached its telling, stands to tell us both of our craving for mutuality and of its satisfaction. It provides us with a fundamental form to represent all the possibilities of experiencing and uttering a human "we." By drawing us to see, in concrete form, now this one, now that one, of our basic human communalities, narrative reminds us how the bonds of mutual trust and shared understanding give our practices, institutions, and forms of life their properly human shape. Within our practices, institutions, and forms of life, therefore, our cravings take on meaning and are appropriately fulfilled according to their possibility for measuring up to this properly human shape: their capability for enabling, for each and for all, full and abiding participation in human mutuality, shaped by bonds of trust and shared understanding.

Through narrative, though not through it alone, imagination allows the truth of our mortality and our finitude to touch us in a way our initial fear of this truth gives us little reason to expect: it gives, and sustains us in, confidence that our most fundamental human hope for the moral future — the full mutuality of human community — will be accomplished. It affords us confidence, paradoxically, in proportion to the clarity with which the particular narrative represents our inability to effect such full mutuality by our own efforts. The oft-told tales are these: though we cannot effect it, it comes; it comes, not in proportion to our efforts, yet still not capriciously; when it fails to come, we are lost, no matter what else we have at our disposal; when it fails to come, we still seek it and hope for it, until the end of our days; when it comes, it is ours to enjoy, so long as we do not try to cling to it and to master it. All these hint at the full truth that comes as gift. It is a truth we marked out before, and now we may properly call it the truth of narrative: history is the will of a just God who knows us.

Narrative invites us to come to know ourselves as God knows us: seekers for the abiding utterance of a "we" that holds together without destroying "I" and "you" for each and all who utter it. As seekers for a "we," aware of our inability to effect by our own power the fulness of mutuality, we are made ready to listen attentively to the truth that narrative offers: such fulness of mutuality will come. It can be relied upon for shaping our lives. It will come — as gift — because history is the will of a just God who knows us, and knows us most fully in our search to utter "we." This God knows us most fully in our search to utter "we" because it is at his initiative that we search. In this search, we have been marked by mutuality, the fundamental sign of God's transcendence as it touches our human existence.[14]

Transformation of Reason: The Context of Practice

Our utterance of "we" has the accents of reason: reason can govern human conduct only in the context of a "world" — a framework to provide a public and common realm to be shared by those who utter "we." The world in which reason is enabled to govern conduct rightly is one that the exercise of our human freedom in the service of mutuality makes both possible and real. Freedom makes this world possible and real by shaping our conduct to keep the promise, made in the acknowledgment we give to human likeness, that we are to go on together. The practices of going on together, which the exercise of our freedom shapes, give us confidence to utter "we."

It was Kant's account of human freedom that provided a particularly useful concept for tracing our search for the utterance of an abiding "we" back to the exercise of our freedom: reason's world-constructing interest that orders the exercise of freedom to the service of human mutuality. His account then notes, however, that even though we can trace our search back to its ground

in freedom, awareness of the finitude of our reason and our conduct require us to place constraints upon the power of philosophical considerations to account for the ordering of freedom to mutuality. These constraints limit our efforts to provide an account
of our human search to utter an abiding "we" in the forms of
discursive reasoning. Yet even in the face of these limitations upon
the account we give of freedom, Kant's critical theory does not
require us to place a limit upon the expectations we articulate
as hopes for the outcome of our search for the utterance of an
abiding "we." Kant allows us to articulate these expectations in
accord with that form of the exercise of reason he terms "moral
faith." As seekers for a "we," aware of our inability to effect by
our own power the fulness of mutuality, we are nonetheless allowed, and even required, to listen attentively to the message
that moral faith propounds: fulness of mutuality, the condition
for an abiding utterance of a "we," will come. We can rely upon
its coming as we try to give moral shape to our lives through
conduct acknowledging, and in service to, mutuality.

This reliance upon the coming of the moral future in the form
of the conditions that provide for an abiding utterance of "we"
marks out what I take to be the logical space that Kant provides
for acknowledgment of God's transcendence.[15] It is within this
space that we can and, indeed, must articulate our hopes about
the outcome of our search for the utterance of an abiding "we."
The forms in which we articulate these hopes are ones we may
rightly call the representations of religious imagination. It is
within this space that reason is rendered capable of transformation into imagination. When so transformed, it enables us to see
that our conduct, shaped by the ordering of freedom to mutuality,
has rendered us open to be touched by the power that enables
that ordering to be at all: God's transcendence, manifest in a
constantly offered invitation to share in his own mutuality. Once
we are so touched, the transformation of reason into imagination achieves its goal: it renders it possible for us to respond to
God's transcendence in the freedom of faith. That faith makes
us aware that the completion of mutuality that our conduct seeks
to effect is made possible only in virtue of God's power to effect
it in abiding form in the moral future.

I have already noted that narrative forms a context in which
the transformation of reason into imagination can be reflectively

accomplished. Narrative provides for the reflective completion of this transformation, which started, in fact, with our initiation into practices of human mutuality. These practices initiate this transformation. They function to put us in the presence of the human mutuality for whose completion freedom enables us to hope. In that hope comes the invitation to stand before God's transcendence. God's transcendence can be made manifest to us as we engage in the practices by which we concretely carry on our search for the conditions that enable us to utter "we." God's transcendence becomes manifest as the initiative at whose behest we search, and in the power that gives assurance that this search will reach its completion: a sharing with one another in the abiding presence of God's mutuality, of which the ordering of our moral freedom to mutuality is pledge and promise.

Practices that render us open to the presence of transcendence are, in the first instance, the patterns of human interaction that place us before one another as centers of action and of value. These are the practices we have already noted as the ones that first call upon the engagement of our freedom in its fundamental mutuality. These practices not only call upon our power in freedom to acknowledge, and to act in virtue of, our human likenesses and mutuality; they also call upon our freedom to bind us together for the future, in virtue of that same acknowledgment. The entrance we make into human mutuality through the exercise of our freedom, therefore, has two aspects: acknowledgment of who and what we most fundamentally are—interdependent human persons—and commitment to be guided by that acknowledgment as we go on together into the future; come what may, a freely acknowledged mutuality holds us bound to each other. This entrance into mutuality brings both light and darkness: the light of a self-understanding that who we are rests upon our interdependence, and the darkness of binding oneself in trust to others for a mutual shaping and sharing of the human future.

These practices begin to render us open to the presence of transcendence by engaging our freedom to the service of mutuality in its concrete human forms. This engagement of our freedom prepares us for a transformation of reason into that power of imagination through which, and only through which, we can be touched by the moral world in the full power of its reality. In virtue of this transformation, the world we could previously represent just as pledge of the moral future—that is, in anticipation of its becoming real,—we can now represent as "gift"—that is, real in the present, as the enabling power for shaping human conduct in fidelity to the pledge of mutuality and the promise of full attainment of human community.

Practice: Opening to Transcendence

The opening to transcendence that the practices of mutuality offer is precarious. Our engagement in patterns of human interaction does not guarantee that we will take note of this opening, or that we will be moved to further engage our freedom toward it. This is so because our reason, as finite, under the importunings of our cravings, can judge that there is no need for us to be bound in mutuality to and for the future. There is no need, because such self-binding is a venture into a darkness that cannot be illumined before we venture forth. We noted this earlier: prior to the exercise of our reason as practical—that is, as the power of governing our conduct in service of mutuality—we have no sureness of the ordering of the freedom to mutuality: even in its exercise, we remain ever capable of concealing from ourselves, in the name of reason, the ordering of freedom to mutuality. We invoke the name of reason for such concealment under the title of "interests." Under this title we place reason in service of the satisfaction of our cravings. Under the title of "interest" we pursue concerns that need not be put to the service of mutuality, but that we nonetheless call reasonable, because they serve to satisfy our particular cravings.

Even when our practices allow the exercise of freedom to disclose its ordering to mutuality, this does not of itself constitute us fully open to transcendence—that is, to be touched by the invitation to share in the mutuality of God's own life. Openness to mutuality with one another is a prelude—a sign that we take our acknowledgment of likeness to one another to be also a pledge to venture on together in expectation of the full achievement of human community. We can be rendered fully open to God's transcendence, however, only by a further venture, which goes beyond even our original venturing forth in the freedom of moral endeavor into practices of human mutuality. This new venture is that of the freedom of faith: the acceptance of the gift of

God's mutuality. Prior to this venture, the full significance of our hope for the attainment of human destiny, made real to us as gift through God's invitation, can remain hidden to us even as we exercise our freedom in service of mutuality.

This venture of the freedom of faith becomes possible when we are called upon to bind ourselves in an unqualified way to mutuality in and for the future. This call is made upon us in those practices of mutuality that disclose that God's response to human mutuality is, has been, and will continue to be unqualified. These are the practices by which we have been, and continue to be, called and constituted as God's own people — as church.[16]

Freedom of Faith: God's Response to Human Mutuality

This call to an unqualified response requires more of our freedom than is in its power as practical reason. As practical reason, freedom can bind us to the future only in a qualified measure: in the mode of expectation, measured in accord with the fidelity of our adherence to the principles of rightly governed conduct.[17] This expectation provides a basis for an opening to transcendence. But this opening is qualified by an awareness of the finitude of our conduct. Insofar as this opening depends upon the efficacy of our moral conduct for the attainment of abiding good, the future to which we pledge ourselves by adherence to these principles is ever beyond our reach.

As pledge issuing from our freedom, therefore, the full achievement of human community is in the darkness of the future. It remains beyond the power of our present conduct in service of mutuality to illumine that darkness. It is beyond our power to adhere in an unqualified way to the pledge our freedom makes for the enduring and full attainment of human community.

As gift, bestowed out of God's transcendence, however, the full attainment of human community presents itself as a light illumining the darkness into which we venture when we exercise our freedom to shape our present conduct to the service of mutuality. As gift, the full achievement of human community renders us open to transcendence in a manner for which the expectation of human destiny grounded in freedom provides the merest hint. As gift, it provides not just an anticipatory open-

ness to the power of transcendence to effect for the future the
full attainment of human community; it provides an openness
by which we can acknowledge as well the irruption of transcendence in the present and the past to effect in us confidence in
the abiding attainment of that destiny.

The actuality of such irruptions escapes reason in its form of
discursive understanding. Even in its practical guise — that is, as
freedom — reason cannot represent the full attainment of human
community as present for us in the world of what is. Such presence is not an element of the world that is within the power of
reason, even as practical, to construct. When the full attainment
of human community is made present to us as gift, reason falls
silent and human freedom senses its powerlessness. Yet this silence and powerlessness are signs that the transformation of reason has begun. In silence and powerlessness, reason can be transformed into the imaginative power that apprehends that we stand
receptive before the presence of the full attainment of human
community when it is offered as gift. This imaginative power
apprehends that the mutuality of freedom is foundational for
the faith that gives direction to the enterprise of moral theology.
The transformation of reason to this imaginative power begins
with attentiveness to those moments in the practices of human
mutuality that tell of how we can be gifted with the communality
of a human destiny to the fulness of mutuality.[18]

These moments come into being through our unqualified engagement in practices of mutuality that can both anticipate the
presence of transcendence and exhibit its actuality in past and
present. These practices are ones that in their ordering to the
service of even the simplest elements of human mutuality, allow
the anticipation and the presence of transcendence — that is, the
invitation to share in God's mutuality — to coalesce into images
that refract in multifarious ways the basic tale of human destiny
met in narrative, as it is told, listened to, and lived. The images
are themselves multiple and many-faceted. They can be familial
and they can be cosmic: parent, creator; they can instance inti-
macy and they can instance power: bride, judge. They each provide a refraction of the truth that narrative claims to tell: history
is the will of a just God who knows us.

The practices of mutuality, which both anticipate of the presence of transcendence and exhibit of its actuality in past and

present, properly delineate the possibility of a religious way of living. As forms of mutuality, they are rooted in freedom. In most instances they are the practices of our ordinary living that exhibit our past and present loyalties and our venturesomeness for the future based upon these loyalties. They delineate the possibilities for a religious way of living insofar as they disclose for us the partial character of our loyalties and the precarious state of our venturesomeness. Even as we deepen our loyalties, we become all too aware of the possibilities of misplacing them; we realize how deeply rooted is our preference not to be asked to risk all for them. Even in the face of our best efforts, our loyalties remain in a partial and precarious state as a result of our human finitude and history.

The tension between our efforts to root our loyalties securely in the service of mutuality and our awareness of their ever partial and precarious state provides an energizing power for the formation of images of mutuality; it allows us to form images to refract the narratives that touch our awareness of human communality at a most fundamental level. This is the level at which we can be touched by the full implications of our craving for mutuality: this craving comes as gift, but we are powerless to satisfy it in due measure by our own efforts. If it has, nonetheless, a satisfaction, this too comes as gift. For our reason and our freedom, darkness surrounds this implication. Our reason and our freedom have already been stretched to their limits by exercising them to represent, for the sake of shaping conduct, our cravings as gifts, and to represent their satisfaction, in the form of the highest good, as hope for the moral future. To represent satisfaction of our cravings not merely as expectation for the moral future, but as gift by whose presence we may even now be touched, is to stretch reason and freedom beyond their limits. These images and the narratives they refract make it possible for us to have our freedom and reason so stretched because they call upon us to exercise them in the guise of imagination.

Freedom of Faith:
Imagination Graced with the Capacity for Truth

We stretch our reason and our freedom into the power of imagination when we represent the satisfaction of our fundamental human craving for mutuality in its most radical possibility: that even when our loyalties have been misplaced, or have not been kept, or have failed to make us venture further along the way of going on together, this craving will be satisfied. The most radical form of the possibility for the satisfaction of our human craving for mutuality is that it comes, always and simply, as gift.

This possibility is not merely "made up" by imagination. If it were, we could not assert it to be true; our representation of it would merely indicate the depth of the human craving for mutuality. But we must, in virtue of our finitude, represent through imagination the satisfaction of our craving for mutuality as gift. This exercise of imagination touches what is true and real because it is rooted in our freedom and our reason, transformed by the acknowledgment of the presence of God's transcendence. This exercise of imagination, formed in hope, therefore, provides us access to what is true.[19] This exercise of imagination is the most fundamental form of our human capacity for approaching what is real in the world of what ought to be and for representing it in its truth. Through imagination we are able to represent the truth of the moral world into which we first venture through the practices of mutuality. This truth is one by which we are transformed. Imagination, and the practices of mutuality in which it has its roots, thus disclose the transforming power of this truth: the concrete presence of God's transcendence. That truth is that there has been, and continues to be, a response to human mutuality that is unqualified because it is God's. The concrete form of God's response is the call to be constituted in mutuality, in the name of Jesus Christ, as church. This unqualified response of God — the call to be a people formed in the power of Christ's name — constitutes the full attainment of human community, not just as an expectation for the moral future, but as a power in the present, to shape our conduct in accord with that attainment.

Practices of human mutuality render us fully open to being touched by the power of transcendence, therefore, when they disclose to us that the first response to mutuality has been, is, and will be an unqualified one. These practices can make it possible for us to see that the first response to the prospect of going on together on the basis of human likeness has not been our own, but God's. They can make it possible for us to see that this response is so totally a gift that it has the power to make our response as well an unqualified one. The unqualified response to our mutuality is the gift of its fulness, made actual to us now in a mode that suits our present incompleteness. This mode is what Christian theology has called "grace."[20]

Our practices manifest the presence of grace when they make it possible to adumbrate unqualified responses to human mutuality in its concrete circumstances. They challenge us to imagine what the world ought to be if God's response to our mutuality became our response to each other. Such adumbration takes many forms. It remains, in most cases, an adumbration rather than a fully detailed picture as a consequence of our fundamental powerlessness to sustain, on our own, efforts for an unqualified response. It is, therefore, sketched out as an ideal: sometimes exhibited in the lives and the conduct of concrete persons; sometimes instanced as exemplary tasks or as paradigmatic deeds; at still other times exhibited in institutionalized procedures that encourage, from generation to generation, participation in the hope and effort to live more closely to an ideal of unqualified response to human mutuality.

These practices adumbrate the possibilities for unqualified responses to mutuality in the concrete forms of our conduct. These responses can be unqualified because they are based upon the response to our mutuality that has been disclosed to us as not our own, as unqualified, and as total gift. Such an unqualified response presents the exercise of our freedom with possibilities it can represent only as risk prior to making such a response. The central risk involves the possibilities for the transformation of human freedom and human reason through such a response. Freedom and reason run the risk of their own destruction and death if an unqualified response to human mutuality is given. Such an unqualified response binds us to go on together, come what may. Going on together, come what may, is a risk, even to the point of destruction and death for our freedom and our reason, because it requires abandonment of the possibility that stands as the final ground of opposition to the acknowledgment of our finitude and mutuality. That possibility is for human self-sufficiency. It is a possibility we find ourselves cherishing because it represents a hope that has bewitching power for freedom and reason when they have been rendered unmindful of God's transcendence. This hope is for the overcoming of our finitude.[21]

We can cherish this hope despite the acknowledgment we make, by the exercise of freedom and reason, of the finitude of our conduct. Our cherishing this hope can be concretely represented in tales of sin, starting from the first that the community of God's people has kept in memory: you shall be as gods. The hope that the acknowledgment of finitude engenders, however, invites no such grasping; it requires, instead, that we wait upon one another, and that we all wait upon God, for the abiding fulfillment of that hope. In the face of that acknowledgment, we nonetheless often exercise our freedom and our reason in ways that show that we have chosen not so to wait, but rather to attempt to bring about the moral future through our own efforts.

The next chapter discusses some of the concrete possibilities that human practices offer for an unqualified response to human mutuality, once our engagement in them takes place in the context of the empowerment of human mutuality by the invitation to share in God's own mutuality. These possibilities do not offer the hope of overcoming finitude; rather, they enable finitude to undergo a transformation that places it at the full service of mutuality. This transformation is one that we can represent with particular aptness in the form of narrative; our finitude becomes of service to mutuality, by its incorporation into the narrative of God's invitation to mutuality, which is unqualified, and which effects the completion of our craving for mutuality: the gift of God's very life, giving glory to our finitude, by enabling each of us to share fully of ourselves, as God shares fully of himself with us.

Freedom of Faith: The Moral World and the Practice of Freedom

My argument to show that the reality of the moral world is constituted in and by the ordering of freedom to mutuality is now complete. It has been completed by showing how the practices of human freedom provide the basis from which imagination exhibits the reality of that world to us. This reality, when first exhibited, is that of human likeness and human mutuality: that we are like one another, and that we can go on with one another. This reality is then exhibited as pledge of the enduring attainment of human community: the world we endeavor to construct through the exercise of our freedom is one that makes an abiding utterance of "we" possible.

By exhibiting, in virtue of the power of imagination, the reality of the moral world, moreover, the practices of human freedom provide for us a foundation for the enterprise of moral theology. The full attainment of human community, which the moral world pledges, lies beyond the power of our conduct to effect. Even so, the practice of human freedom can be represented, especially in image and in story, as empowered by the presence of the full attainment of human community: an abiding "we" has been uttered, and its utterance enables us to continue to go on together.[22]

Our acknowledgment that our ways of going on together are empowered by the utterance of an abiding "we" constitutes the fundamental moment of the freedom of faith. It is an acknowledgment that would be beyond our power to make, were it not offered as a gift: the abiding utterance of a "we" is not first ours; it is God's. Yet it is a "we" so powerful and so unqualified that it is offered for us to utter in our own name, as finite.

Moral theology is the endeavor we make to see and to articulate with greater clarity the ways of going on together that are empowered by the abiding utterance of a "we." This is the endeavor I take up, in an illustrative, rather than systematic, manner in the next, and final, chapter. These concrete ways of exhibiting the reality of the moral world should provide further clarification of the steps taken in the argument I have elaborated to establish the exercise of human freedom as the foundation for the enterprise of moral theology.

5. Hope, Community, and Worship: Images of Christian Freedom

In this chapter I shall indicate some consequences that the argument I have presented for the ordering of freedom to mutuality has for ways we may understand the moral significance of, and give moral shape to, concrete human practices. The treatment given here to specific areas of conduct is not intended to be exhaustive of all the moral dimensions that can be uncovered from either a philosophical or a theological perspective. I hope, instead, to single out with some clarity some instances that manifest our contemporary failure to see the moral core of human practices: their possibility for making manifest the ordering of human freedom to the service of mutuality. This failure, in my judgment, is basically a failure of imagination. It has its origin in what I term, in Chapter 1, the mistake about the character of freedom that has become embedded in our contemporary self-understanding: we conceive of freedom principally in terms of its reference to human agents in their individuality and independence, rather than in terms of their shared communalities and their fundamental interdependence.

This way of understanding freedom has had serious consequences for the very terms in which moral issues have been posed. In particular, the moral status of the individual's choice has been made to occupy center stage, whereas the public realm in which and for which that choice is made has faded so far into the background that it has effectively been lost from view. It is my judgment that discussion of some moral issues has reached an impasse because we have been at times unable, and at other times unwilling, to consider the possibility of simply seeing ourselves, as moral agents, and the matters of our conduct, from a perspective other than that of choice.[1]

In the course of the preceding three chapters, I have presented a case for seeing things from another perspective. This case has been offered, not to deny value to human individuality and independence, or to reduce the moral significance of choice, but to place their value back into the context of our finitude. In various ways, many centuries of Western philosophy and of Christian theology affirmed finitude to be definitive of our human condition, but we, in the present century, seem to have lost it from view. I have, moreover, focused this case upon what I take to be a central mark of our finitude: our interdependence. We each stand in need of one another. All of us stand in need of God. And, most mysterious of all, God, by inviting us to share in the mutuality of divine life, and by enabling human realities to stand as effective signs to bestow and to nourish that life, has taken on a commitment to stand in need of us as instruments and witnesses of that life.

Now that a case for this perspective has been made, I propose to consider some of the consequences this different way of seeing freedom has for the way we can describe and deal with some of the moral issues that have occupied our attention in recent years. The proposals I shall make with regard to particular issues are offered in remedy of the failure of imagination to see freedom as anything else but the individual's power of choice. They are suggestions to gain imaginative purchase upon our human practices so that, by their disclosure of the ordering of freedom to mutuality, we may set these issues within the context of the fundamental reality of the moral world.

I. TIME, FIDELITY, AND PUBLIC PROMISE

Marriage: Private Choice, Public Promise

Contemporary patterns of marriage and family life in the United States have been the subject of widespread journalistic coverage, scholarly study, and government concern in recent years. Perhaps the single item upon which almost all concerned could agree is that the current situation of the family — which some, quite rightly in my view, see as a situation of crisis — is the outcome of a large set of diverse and complex factors. As a result, an attempt to offer, as I plan to do here, a set of unifying concepts as a way of gaining entrance to central moral dimensions of this situation runs the risk of oversimplification. The risk is lessened, however, if we keep in mind that one function of the imaginative unification (that is, "world-construction") proper to the moral use of reason is to bring out in stark relief those elements of our human practices upon which, usually little by little, we stake our lives.

I am proposing here a general understanding of the moral dimensions of the practices of marriage and family life. Without such a general understanding, we shall find ourselves at a loss in making moral assessments of particular instances of these practices. My proposal is that we fashion our understanding in accord with images of the public realm that allow us to specify particular ways in which human mutuality grounded upon freedom functions at the core of these practices. I hope to show that, in particular, images of the public realm that adequately disclose the mutuality of freedom would enable us to specify the mutuality of marriage and family life in terms of the public pledge to care for one another's total well-being in human time. One consequence of this specification of mutuality in the practices of marriage and family life is that fidelity is thereby empowered to stand within these practices as an achievement of public moral significance.[2]

It is only fair to note that my effort here to establish an understanding of the moral dimensions of marriage and family in terms of mutuality and the public realm has a polemical side. It is offered as a counterweight to what I perceive as a factor that has increasingly shaped the perception, in late twentieth-century American culture, of basic social institutions and practices: the rhetoric of freedom as privatized individual choice. When that rhetoric is taken seriously as a guide to practice, it undercuts the possibility for a shared image of a truly public realm to be a way of understanding human social practices. Its impact upon the understanding of marriage and family in our culture has been such, in my judgment, that we are faced with the curious social situation of the increasing "privatization" of marriage and family. We seem to have arrived at the paradoxical situation of being unable to articulate a public, shareable, human meaning for a basic human social reality: the promising, bonding, child-rearing, heritage-regulating institutions and practices we speak of as marriage and family.

I believe it is also important to note the difference between, on the one hand, the necessity I am claiming for a public context of meaning to provide moral intelligibility for human social practices and, on the other hand, the adequacy of the moral intelligibility provided by a particular public context. It may well be the case that the unreflective public context of meaning in the United States, which provided moral intelligibility for practices of marriage and family life through the middle of this century, could be judged on many counts inadequate. This judgment, however, does not require that we abandon public contexts altogether; it surely requires that we work to fashion a more adequate one.

What I term a public context for the moral intelligibility of the practices of marriage and family should not be thought of as coextensive with or equivalent to its civic or legal contexts. We have retained the latter, but in keeping with the rhetoric of freedom as private choice, we have generally managed to eliminate all possibilities of their functioning as elements contributing to moral intelligibility. They function instead, in the case of marriage, to regulate, according to a standard of civic fairness, the more notable consequences for society of what is simply assumed to be, in terms of its moral significance, the private choice made by two individuals. This stands in direct contrast to the moral intelligibility that an image of the public realm, adequate for disclosing the mutuality of freedom, would confer; it would make it possible for us to understand marriage, not as a private choice made in public, with social effects, but as a major paradigm of public choice. It is, in fact, a paradigm of the public choice that founds human community as a moral reality. This is so inasmuch as it gives us a clear focus, through an unreserved and explicit pledge exchanged by two persons, upon the fundamental object of that founding choice: care for one another's well-being.

Fidelity: The Pledge to Care in Human Time

The rhetoric of freedom as private choice does not allow this choice, among others, to be paradigmatic of the fundamentally public character of human moral reality. The rhetoric of freedom presents us with a beguiling picture of human moral reality. It is beguiling inasmuch as it offers a way to extricate oneself, in each choice one makes, from a condition essential to the human moral universe as it can be constituted by images of the public realm. This condition is time, which in our modern age we have begun to understand as taking its public shape for humanity in the guise of history.

The rhetoric of freedom does not allow the human pledge constitutive of marriage to be conceived as a morally significant feature of the public narrative of human existence we have learned to call history. In the rhetoric of freedom, marriage and family are paradigmatic domains of privacy; though they are certainly not insulated from the shaping forces of history, they are, curiously enough, denied power to give shape to history.[3]

The suggestion I have for fashioning a general understanding of the moral dimensions of the practices constituting marriage and family is that we have the imagination to picture things differently. In particular, I suggest that we begin to find ways for understanding marriage and family as a public pledge to endeavor with a community to shape the moral future. Such a pledge, moreover, presupposes the community's willingness and ability to envision a shared moral future and to strive toward it. This underlines the fact that the possibility of being able to conceive differently the moral intelligibility of the practices of marriage and family is directly tied to the possibility of picturing a public realm adequate to disclose human mutuality. In order for those who enter marriage to see, as a major element of its moral significance, that it pledges them to endeavor with the community to shape the moral future, the community must itself be able to see and to articulate ways that its mutuality in the present discloses its hopes for the moral future. The community must do the same in order to sustain practices of family living as pledges and participation in the shaping of the moral future.

Commitment and Community: Practices for Sustaining Hope

Practices of marriage and family life have been notable victims of the increasing difficulty of sustaining hope for the moral future. Symptomatic of this difficulty is the doubt, present not only among the young, that is often voiced about the possibility of a lifelong commitment. As this doubt is usually expressed, its resolution is all too often presumed to rest solely upon the personal moral resources of the persons entering into the commitment. In the face of the uncertainties of the future, honest self-awareness of the particular human inconstancies to which one is prone can make lifelong commitment appear an impossible ideal. Inasmuch as the commitment is mutual, moreover, each person is also asking the other to sustain hope in the face of the other's inconstancy, as well as his or her own. This adds to the appearance of impossibility.[4]

The general understanding I am proposing would have us raise the question of lifelong commitment against a different background. We should not look solely to the personal moral resources of those entering into the commitment; we must look to resources that particular human communities have the responsibility to provide so that a hope engendering patterns of fidelity can be sustained. Indeed, without such resources, it hardly seems possible that the personal moral resources requisite for lives of fidelity can be aroused and flourish.

The grim judgment that has to be made about late-twentieth-century American culture is that it has increasingly failed in its responsibility as a moral community to sustain the hope that engenders patterns of fidelity. One reason for this may be the simple fact that patterns of American culture have become so shaped by the pursuit of particular interests that they cannot cohere into the shape of a moral community. There are, however, some positive signs that particular communities, which have been more successful in retaining an identity as moral communities, have started to become more explicitly aware of their responsibility for sustaining the kind of hope that makes patterns of fidelity possible. An instance of this can be found in efforts within the Catholic Church to institute more comprehensive programs of marriage preparation. Crucial to the long-term success of these programs, however, will be the extent to which not just those participating in them, but also each particular community and parish of Catholics, become aware of their shared responsibility as community to be a locus of hope for marriage and family life. The community must be a source of countervailing weight, in its attitudes and practices, to those elements of the contemporary ethos — whether social, economic, psychological, or political — that so restrict the significance of experience to the satisfaction of present needs that long-term fidelity and loyalty become unintelligible as sources for the governance of conduct. For a community to exert such countervailing weight, moreover, it must be able to articulate the images that disclose the core of its identity, and to mark off in a critical and reflective fashion the implications that these images have for shaping human practices. For a Christian community, among these images will be the reign or kingdom of God, covenant, the body of Christ, and church; each image takes a role in the reflective disclosure of the mutuality of freedom proper to the practices of marriage and family life.

My suggestion, therefore, is that the current situation with regard to marriage and family life requires that particular communities look to their symbolic and imaginative representations of community identity in order to locate their basic moral understandings of these and other human social practices. It is from these representations that images of a public realm can be articulated. It is these images that must then pass the critical test of being able to disclose the specific mutuality of freedom functioning at the core of these practices. If they pass this test, they then provide a basis on which the community can refine or refashion practices that have been failing to exhibit adequately the mutuality at their core.

My suggestion has its most immediate bearing upon communities that have maintained the tools and the skills to determine and articulate reflectively the symbolic and imaginative representations of their community identity. Among those tools and skills I include philosophy, theology, literature, and art. To make my suggestion effective, moreover, these tools and skills must be applied not only to bring to light these symbolic and imaginative representations, but also to test their degree of adequacy for entering into the construction of a public ethos in a presently fragmented world.

Covenant: The Initiative of God's Mutuality

The importance of testing the adequacy of symbolic and imaginative representations of community identity can be seen by illustrating the way in which one such symbolic representation functions to disclose mutuality. My illustration is the symbolic representation "covenant." Covenant discloses for a Christian community a mutuality at the core of its existence of which it is not and can never claim to be the source. What is offered in this mutuality, moreover, is a share in God's own life. This mutuality is constituted as a possibility for the community not in virtue of its own endeavor, but in virtue of the initiative of God's promise. Covenant also stands as a symbol of hope insofar as the community perceives that in its history this promise has been sustained by God's fidelity even in the face of human inconstancy. In general, covenant functions to situate members of a Christian community in a public realm of God's promises. It stands more particularly as an image that discloses fidelity as central to the character of the mutuality involved in the human promise to sustain a shared life of care for one another.[5]

The image of covenant, therefore, may be able to sustain a hope that engenders practices of fidelity in marriage and family life for a particular community whose fundamental identity can be reflectively acknowledged in this image. Such reflective acknowledgment of an image expressive of a community's identity has become uncommon in our literal-minded age. A critical set of questions for these practices in late-twentieth-century America can and should be formulated, therefore, to initiate such reflection. First, do we have left to us any symbolic representations of our identity as a moral, civic, economic, and political community from which we can articulate an image of the public realm? Secondly, if, as seems most probable, we do not, how then might the specific sustaining images — for example, covenant — of particular communities function in efforts to fashion anew an image of the public realm that all can share? These questions lead directly to a second area of moral concern that the main argument of this volume can address: the necessity of fashioning a notion of a "common good."

II. WANTS, IMAGINATION, AND THE COMMON GOOD

Rights, Wants, and Human Good

There is probably no issue in public debate more in need of understanding from the perspective of a notion of "common good," and less likely to receive it, than that of abortion. A principal reason for this can be found in the terms in which the discussion has been set: it is taken without further reflection that the core moral, legal, and political issues almost without exception have to do with "rights" — their existence, their conflict, and the extent to which their exercise is to be protected and supported in public policy.[6]

It would be foolish to deny that talk of rights offers an important way to understand what is morally at stake both in specific instances of abortion and in the social and political conditions under which it has become readily available. It would be equally foolish, however, to think that talk of rights offers the only, or even the most illuminating, way to understand all that abortion puts morally at stake. A particularly tragic consequence of casting discussion of abortion almost exclusively in terms of rights has been that it makes it all too easy for parties on every side of the issue to practice an especially pernicious form of moral self-deception. Talk about rights makes it possible to place demands upon the public realm that, when they are met, give shape to practices of the life we share with one another in the workplace, the marketplace, the polity, the neighborhood, and even in the home. As talk about rights has been framed in discussions of abortion, however, it has generally precluded the possibility of submitting to serious public assessment the understanding of human good presupposed in such demands. The discussion does not require us to spell out, let alone put to the test of public assessment, the human good of the shape that the life we share with each other will take as a result of meeting these demands.

The possibility for this kind of self-deception is most notable in the curious function served by a term that is so often used but so little analyzed in the discussion: "unwanted," as in "unwanted pregnancy." This term has proved particularly useful in forestalling efforts to introduce into public discussion assessments of the understandings of human good at stake in the practice of abortion. Few persons seem willing to argue that very many, let alone all, "unwanted pregnancies" are, without qualification, good. The term nonetheless encourages self-deception to enter into the discussion because it allows us to gloss over the fact that it might be important for the formation both of moral judgment and of public policy to subject to assessment the reasons offered for judging a particular pregnancy or type of pregnancy "unwanted."

The reasons offered are numerous and varied. They range from a judgment of immediate danger to a woman's life, through considerations for the well-being or the economic prospects of the family, to the inconvenience of interrupting a career or disrupting a personal relationship. Whatever the particular reason or types of reasons may be, most, if not all of them, presuppose some judgment about the kind of human good that ought to be served by the human practices and institutions already ingredient in the situation. For instance, patterns of economic opportunity or of economic expectations presumed to be worth pursuing can make particular pregnancies "unwanted." The "good" of marriage and family life is understood variously in our culture: it can be understood to serve as an ideal of self-fulfillment; it can be understood as a partnership to serve career ambitions or social expectations; it can be understood as a partnership fostering a mutual concern for others extending beyond the couple's relationship. The judgment that a pregnancy is "unwanted" in particular cases is one that frequently seems to be made in conjunction with which good one assumes marriage to serve.[7] It is obviously a judgment that is more likely to be made when one takes that good to be simply self-fulfillment than when one takes that good to be a partnership fostering a mutual concern for others extending beyond the couple's relationship. Patterns of sexual conduct, whether inside or outside marriage, are often determined in our culture by presuppositions, not critically examined, about how that conduct serves the psychological "good" or "health" or "integration" of human persons, or the "good" of a particular relationship between persons. These patterns, and the assumptions about good on which they are based, frequently serve as a basis on which a pregnancy is judged "unwanted."

These illustrations should make it clear that a description of a pregnancy as "unwanted" typically carries with it judgments, often made implicitly and uncritically, about the kinds of human good that are at stake in the situation, and that ought to be served in a response to that situation. In consequence, if we hope to provide even a description adequate to the moral dimensions of situations in which abortion is proposed as a possible course of action, we must be willing and able to identify and provide justifications for those judgments about human good that are implied in the use of a term such as "unwanted." The responsibility to spell out such implicit understandings of good and their justifications would seem to hold with even stronger force when such descriptions are offered in processes directed to fashioning sound public policies toward these situations. This is so because public policies have a shaping force upon the forms taken by human practices productive of good.

The Failure of Imagination: Wants Empowered to Shape Good

As long as discussion of abortion is framed principally or exclusively in terms of rights, however, hopes for descriptions of these situations adequate for purposes of moral assessment or of public policy-formation cannot be met. This is so because there is a particular picture of human interaction that provides the background of moral intelligibility for much of the rights talk that has dominated discussions of abortion. According to this picture, the form of human interaction of primary and paradigmatic moral significance takes place in pressing and acknowledging claims upon each other in virtue of needs and wants. There are versions of this picture in which one of the results of this form of interaction is the recognition or construction of a genuinely common human good, to which each and all have a share and claim, and which serves as a criterion for assessing particular claims made by individuals or by groups upon the public realm. These versions of this picture, however, have generally been lost from sight in late-twentieth-century practices of pressing claims upon each other and upon the public realm. In their place is more and more a picture in which the common good that can emerge from interaction has ceased to be normative. It has become, without qualification, the aggregate total of satisfied claims.

The loss of an effective normative force for the "common good" is, at root, a failure of imagination; we seem less and less able to picture, in an way that can be effective for shaping policy and action, the kind of human good that can be shared by each and all.[8] All the goods that we seek appear to be particular, and even our pursuit of goods that we once might have thought truly universal, such as peace or justice, seem ineluctably skewed by the particularity of our interests: although all of us desire peace, we most eagerly pursue the kind of peace that best advances our particular interests.

The current state of the discussion about abortion provides a test case for our readiness to acknowledge and to attempt to remedy this failure of imagination. There is a pressing need to move discussion to a level from which we can begin to see the implied understandings of good that shape the terms of the debate, the tactics, and the practices advocated by various parties to the discussion. We need to do so in order to identify and to assess the consequences that these understandings of good have for the formation of moral judgments and for the shaping of public policy. To move discussion to this level, however, parties to it will have to embark upon a critical and, thereby, painful process of articulating for themselves and for the public at large the implied understandings of good that are at the core of their positions and the strategies they have used to make them effective in the public realm. I call the process painful because such a critical exercise is likely to reveal not only deep particularisms in understandings of good that have been assumed to be universal, but also large inconsistencies among understandings of good presupposed in the principles underpinning the positions advocated, in the strategy and tactics employed in advocacy, and in the public policies and practices taken to be consequences of the positions advocated. Two items in particular that stand in need of such close critical scrutiny are the two values that have functioned as the rhetorical labels for polarizing positions in the discussion: "life" and "choice."

The process of uncovering the understandings of good already at work in the discussion and in the practices upon which the discussion bears may be painful, inasmuch as it is an exercise in self-knowledge. It is, however, not as difficult as a subsequent step needed to move discussion to a level that more adequately discloses the moral implications of the social and political conditions under which abortion has become readily available. This subsequent step is the effort to fashion out of our particularisms a notion of the common good adequate for forming normative judgments upon the pursuit of particular human interests. The particularisms out of which we seek to fashion a notion of "common good" are the images in which are represented the identities of the communities of which we are members. In times when the domain of what was "public" and, thereby, of common interest to all could be considered coincident with the realm of the political and the religious, images representing the identity of communities could be clear and straightforward: kingdom and church; commonwealth and covenant. In our time, the domain of what is public has become so fragmented that there is no particular realm — political, economic, social, or religious — whose identifying image can be considered by all to be reliable for locating the human goods and interests that are truly common.

Moral Imagination: Good and the Recognition of Communality

As a result, what I have termed moral imagination has a crucial role to play in any effort to fashion a notion of common good. Its function within this effort is to draw into the present and the future the possibilities for communality that it has retrieved out of our particularities in the very founding of moral community. The notion of "common good," therefore, may be considered one way of concretely extending, for the sake of assessing and guiding conduct, the recognition of communality at the heart of moral life: "I am as she; she is as I."

This clearly suggests, moreover, that fashioning an understanding of common good adequate for normative purposes will encounter difficulty in proportion to the poverty of our imaginative representations of human communality. The more we find ourselves unable to represent why we might and should say to each and to all, or to this group, or to this one individual, "I am as she; she is as I," so much the more shall we find ourselves at a loss to desire, discover, or fashion a good we would each and all be able to share. And so much the more shall we find ourselves willing to press our interests against these others without constraint.

The argument I have offered for understanding the core of human freedom to consist in the mutuality of a shared moral destiny indicates that a central element of an adequate notion of common good will itself be mutuality. The establishment, the fostering, and the service of human mutuality are thereby to function in giving moral shape to human practices. This function is accomplished to the extent that each and all of our human practices — whether in the workplace, marketplace, polity, or home — are made possible by, and continue the possibility of, shared understanding and mutual trust. There can be little doubt that by this measure many of our human practices have been, and continue to be, marginally moral, both in their shape and in their concrete instances. There is no doubt in my mind that the acceptance of abortion by our contemporary culture has as one of its major engendering factors the massive failure of many of the practices of our social, political, and economic life to establish, foster, and be at the service of human mutuality. The peculiar moral evil of abortion is that in response to these failures it offers only the counsel of despair: we can imagine no better course of action than to prevent this one from entering into the mutuality of our world.

Fashioning a notion of "common good" requires that we be disciplined by moral imagination to seek out our human communalities and to articulate them into hopes for the moral future. These hopes are to provide reliable guidance for shaping our conduct to establish, foster, and serve human mutuality. The fragmentation of the domain of what is public makes it particularly difficult for us to embark in common upon such a discipline of moral imagination. In the situation of fragmentation a governing principle in the domain of what is public has been to express communalities only in their most formal terms. There is no expectation that acceptance of communalities expressed this way will generate a truly shared moral world. Such acceptance will simply make possible a modus vivendi in which the play of interests at the intersection of different moral worlds can be made subject to procedures for the settlement of conflict.

Fragmentation in the public realm is so deep that, in my judgment, the possibility of fostering a discipline of moral imagination has come to rest upon the extent to which particular moral communities can engage themselves both directly and reflectively with the sources that offer and nourish the symbols of their identity. Two of the sources for the identity of Christian communities are Scripture and worship. It may, therefore, very well be the case, as the next section will suggest, that the route to a notion of common good in the public realm has one starting point for Christians in the life of worship that shapes their lives and gives discipline to their moral imagination.

III. WORSHIP, IMAGINATION, AND A SHARED WORLD

Worship: Human Destiny to Mutuality

The route from worship to a notion of common good that would be able to function normatively for the public realm is not direct; nor is it a route along which I should expect everyone to travel. The guide along this route is moral imagination. The steps along the route to be taken here will bring only to some of the signs posted by imagination; they do not traverse the path to its end.

Moral imagination serves as guide insofar as it is through its empowerment that we are first enabled to recognize our human communalities as a force for shaping conduct. Worship can serve as the starting point for a route to a normative notion of common good inasmuch as in it our imagination is empowered to recognize the most fundamental and overarching human communality: a shared destiny to participate in the mutuality of the life of God.[9] When worship empowers imagination in terms of human destiny, it opens up for a community the possibility of representing the full shape and extent of human mutuality. It is in virtue of such representation that a normative notion of common good can begin to take form.

Along this route from worship to the common good we can gain a prospect on the significance that changes in the forms of Catholic public worship have for an understanding of moral conduct from the ambit of faith. From this prospect we should be able to note that even though these changes have, for many, apparently shattered a shared world, they have done so in consequence of an effort to refocus our vision upon the depth and the extent of the public realm to which the destiny to share in the mutuality of God's life commits each and all.

Temporality and Language: Images to Shape a Public Realm

Our human temporality is one aspect of the public realm for which changes in the form of Catholic public worship provide a new focus. Roman Catholic liturgical practice before the Second Vatican Council, particularly in its more solemn forms, provided a prospect upon human temporality by imaging a moment of the timelessness of God's time. We should not underestimate the possibilities that such a prospect has for liberating persons for mutuality with others and with God; yet it nonetheless became in the course of time a prospect from which one easily could take refuge from the requirements of human mutuality both within and without the timelessness of worship.

One way of characterizing the revelation that is offered by the Christian doctrine of the incarnation is that God's timelessness has not taken refuge from the requirements of human mutuality and human temporality. As helpful as a prospect upon human temporality from a moment of the timelessness of God's time may be, it is one that the doctrine of incarnation suggests is not the only prospect that God takes and to which he calls his people. Many of the changes initiated in the forms of Catholic worship since the Second Vatican Council take what I would term an incarnational prospect: they lie open to the requirements of human mutuality and human temporality.

An obvious instance is language: the very suppleness of a living language can be both a blessing and a curse for the composer of liturgical texts. It is a blessing because an ear for its richness will make it possible for God's word to be spoken in the accents of the very life of the people; it is a curse because the stately language of one age can corrode in a later age into pomposity and bombast, and today's language of tender personal affection can find itself transformed tomorrow into sentimental drivel.

Of even larger significance, however, is the way in which changes in the forms of Catholic worship leave open to the requirements of human mutuality and human temporality a community's understanding of itself as a people called together to worship. This, of course, is not something totally new: Christian worship in each generation has served to locate the human world and God's people in their proper mutuality and temporality. It does so insofar as its fundamental form is a call to God's presence and an acknowledgment of him for who he is: Creator, Lord, Savior, Spirit. In the acknowledgment of who God is, who we are is disclosed to us.[10] What may very well be new, at least for this age and culture, is that the forms of worship that the church has fashioned now make it even more unmistakable that the call to God's presence and the call to acknowledge him is also a call to be present to each other and to acknowledge one another as hearers of God's call.

Call to Worship, Call to Mutuality

The call to be present to one another was muted in much of the liturgical practice in the Catholic Church for many decades before the Second Vatican Council. Its much clearer voice in the present forms of the Roman liturgy has produced some ironic, though not altogether surprising, results. Some have attempted to fashion practices in which this call to be present to one another is the only one that can be heard in worship; its source in the call of the transcendent God to be acknowledged as the one who constitutes us as a people able to be fully present to one another is forgotten. Others have tried to retain the earlier forms, sometimes defiantly, perceiving those forms to be the ones that call them to and constitute them in their Catholic identity. They have sensed that new forms of worship can and will empower a people's imagination to see and understand differently who they are before the face of the living God. Cloaked over by defiance is the unease that comes from sensing that this empowerment of imagination to new understanding will demand different ways of living as well. Then there are those whose practice of the new forms has not yet been adequately shaped by comprehension of the call addressed to them through those forms to become more fully God's people through presence to one another; among these may yet be a majority of Catholics in the United States.

The connection that links all these results is the power that worship has to form and to focus the public context of Christian understanding and practice. The changes that have taken place in Catholic liturgical practice must appear, not the least because of the swiftness with which they were put into effect, to have set up a kaleidescopic depiction of the juncture of the human and the sacred in place of a stately, serene, though sometimes stern image of divine mystery. It is nonetheless possible to pick out some of the main items upon which the public context of Catholic life is being refocused through these changes. The one I deem most significant for the enterprise of moral theology is the explicit responsibility for the character of the community's public worship that the renewed liturgy places upon each and all, for each and all.[11] Catholic teaching and practice will continue, no doubt, to apportion this responsibility within an overarching framework of ordained priestly ministry. This should not cause us to forget the fact that the forms of liturgy itself now require that the concrete exercise of this responsibility take shape in a full awareness of human mutuality and human temporality. The practices that can continuously and effectively bring that awareness into each of the community's public celebrations of worship are not easy to devise or to master. As anyone who has participated in a "liturgy planning session" knows, this is not only subject to all the normal pitfalls of human group interaction and the special pitfalls of church group interaction, but it also has to serve all too often as an exercise for learning the most basic elements of this responsibility. In such circumstances, it should not be too surprising that the price such learning initially costs can be embarrassing liturgical disaster.

Particular failures should not distract attention from the decisive refocusing of understanding upon the church's public context that Catholic liturgical reform effects when successfully put into practice. This refocusing centers upon the character of each one's participation in that public context; attendance and attentiveness no longer suffice to mark off the range even of "ordinary" lay participation in luturgical celebration. For a people long unaccustomed to having practices explicitly expressive of mutuality central to the public life of worship and faith, the introduction of such practices can be distressing. It is therefore hardly surprising that the participation envisioned in the renewed forms of Catholic worship has, in many cases, been put into practice simply as a more sophisticated form of attendance and attentiveness.

Though practices can be made routine in a way that smothers the mutuality that should be expressed (for example, a perfunctory greeting of peace), and though they can be made to mute the call to be present to one another (for example, sin and guilt

can be privatized in a reconciliation room as well as in a confes-
sional), their presence in the church's life of worship can and,
I believe, should be seen as a herald of a future of richer understanding and surer expression of the mutuality central to the
freedom of Christian faith. Their presence in the life of worship
should bring into greater prominence those images in which mutuality is the core of the community's self-identity—for example, God's people, the pilgrim church, the servant church. Their
presence can be a central element in the long process of bringing
to ever greater actuality, in each aspect of the community's life,
the mutuality to which God's people are called.

Worship: A Discipline for Moral Imagination

A community whose worship acknowledges and is expressive
of the human mutuality whose origin and destiny is God's own
mutuality has open to it a basic resource for the discipline of moral
imagination. In worship we encounter concrete representations
of our human mutuality of origin and destiny as these have been
shaped in Scripture and in the church's traditions of prayer. With
our imaginations formed by these representations, we can then
cast about for those human communalities that give a sign, however weak, of that origin and destiny. We can then seek to foster
practices that accord public acknowledgment to these communalities and disclose more clearly to the public realm the mutuality of which they are the signs.

This discipline of moral imagination—to seek out the human
communalities that give sign of our origin and destiny in
mutuality—can serve to link the worship of Christian communities to the task of fashioning a notion of common good adequate for normative purposes in the public realm. As noted at
the start of this section, this link is not a direct one; a Christian
community cannot expect to place in the public realm, without
interpretation, the images that have empowered its imagination
to discern human communalities as signs of the presence of God's
mutuality in human origins and destiny. Such a community's
journey toward a notion of common good starts once efforts are
made to represent the communalities that disclose mutuality in
terms that can be understood by those not of the community and
who thus do not yet possess the images that have empowered

the imagination of the Christian community to see these communalities. It must continue its journey in the hope of joining with other communities that are also trying to discipline their imaginations to seek out human communalities in the expectation of a destiny of mutuality.

The journey to a notion of common good in a fragmented public realm is an extremely difficult one. A stock of shared public images expressive of mutuality is no longer available in such a realm. Thus the journey to a common good must start in particularities: images that represent the moral identity of particular communities, in which hope is to be placed that they disclose ever-more-embracing human communalities. Some of these journeys may be doomed from the start: trust may be placed in images too fragile to bear the weight of ever-more-encompassing human communalities; others may go astray, following images decked in the gaudy colors that promise a shortcut to mutuality, but a shortcut that avoids the vulnerabilities to which our communalities subject us. Still others — and this may be by far the majority — never get started, because there are neither means to locate the images that represent and the practices that foster the community's identity, nor the will to test these images and practices for their reliability in disclosing more embracing human communalities.

A fragmented public realm makes it ever more difficult for journeys toward a common good to start. This places a heavy burden of responsibility, therefore, upon communities that can locate the images and the practices that constitute their identity. Ironically, their self-aware particularity can become, in these circumstances, an essential resource for discharging this responsibility. It enables them to embark upon the kind of reflection that clearly articulates these images and carefully assesses practices for their fidelity to them. This reflection is only a first step, of course, and can remain self-enclosed, to be of service only to the community's particular good. It will almost surely remain self-enclosed and, perhaps, divisively sectarian if the community has acquiesced to the fragmentation of the public realm.[12] If, however, the community has an emboldened imagination for the possibilities of human mutuality even in a fragmented public realm, it may be able to take its particularism well beyond sectarianism. It may be able to fashion practices that make its particularism witness to the common good; it may be able to fashion language that compels attention because it points to communalities that all particularisms can acknowledge.

A fundamental way for a Christian community to locate the images and practices that constitute its identity will be through reflective inquiry, in faith, into how it has been, and is being, formed in and through the practices of its worship. It is not my proposal that reflection upon Christian worship should make the fashioning of a notion of common good its principal theme and preoccupation. What I propose, rather, is that Christian worship and, in particular, the worship of the Catholic community of which I am a member, might become constantly more aware of the presence, in the images and the forms of public worship, of God's call to mutuality with him and with each other. Awareness of that call, acceptance and response to that call, can then become a shaping power to make us sensitive, both as individuals and as a church, to the whole range of human communalities that need acknowledgment as the basis for an authentic common good. Awareness of that call can also make us bold enough to propose for consideration, even by a fragmented world, the practices that will effectively bring closer, for each and all, full enjoyment of a common good.

IV. CERTAINTY, IMAGINATION, AND MORAL PRACTICE

Moral Education in a Fragmented Public Realm

The three areas of conduct discussed so far in this chapter all point to the form that the basic contemporary challenge to moral imagination takes: the fragmentation of a public realm in which our multiple social contexts can intersect for the fashioning of a common good. In the face of such fragmentation, imagination must be emboldened to represent the images of human mutuality that urge and invite each and all of us into a shared and shareable world. I have indicated that imagination can be so emboldened by the disclosure of the human mutuality that stands at the core of the exercise of freedom. Fragmentation of the public realm makes it difficult to embolden imagination because the practices that contribute to and perpetuate the fragmentation resist the disclosure of mutuality in the exercise of freedom.

This resistance has a paradoxical manifestation in an apparently flourishing contemporary concern for moral education. This concern has its origin in a variety of sources. It generates a paradox, however, whenever these sources are set at variance with a central and necessary goal of moral education: to discipline imagination to a vision adequate to the full dimensions of human mutuality. In a fragmented public realm, many sources even of the most sincere concern for moral education can be set at variance with this goal. This is so because such circumstances force the vision of each social context — familial, political, economic, religious, and the like — to be, in principle, truncated to the measure of interests particular to that context.

I do not propose to assess the whole range of sources of concern for moral education as to their congruence or variance with the specific goal of moral education that I have formulated. I will look just at one, which I suspect is paradigmatic of an extensive segment of this range. I have selected it because it captures what I think is still a dominant expectation for moral education among many parents and educators in Christian communities, even though it is an expectation for which the practices of moral education can offer no guarantee of fulfillment.

The social context from which this particular concern arises is one that I should term familial; it is a concern for the rectitude of personal conduct. Not infrequently this concern has an even more particular focus: the rectitude of sexual conduct. A fragmented public realm makes it possible for this concern to function in a way at variance with the goal of moral education: it can function to obscure or even to block vision of the human mutuality at the core of freedom. The particular way this concern manifests its paradoxical character for moral education is that it can require the abandonment of practices essential for the discipline of moral imagination: the probing of principles and practices for their adequacy in fashioning, fostering, and protecting human mutuality for each and for all.

The concrete manifestations of this concern that put the moral educator under pressure to abandon the discipline of moral imagination are themselves paradoxical. There is, on the one hand, the demand that moral education provide "right answers" that will be ready at hand for a variety of moral situations. Not too many years ago, this was a demand heard most often from the parental and adult world; now it is not uncommon for students themselves to voice it. On the other hand, there is the demand for recognizing the unassailability of feeling as the final criterion for the rectitude of personal conduct. Although the clamor of this demand among students has now become more subdued, its sound does not come only from that quarter; it gets played in sophisticated variation in movements to give privatized choice an ever-increasing field of options.[13]

Mutuality: Education for Critical Moral Judgment

Both demands require suspension of the kind of critical moral dialogue whose essential condition is commitment to mutuality as the locus of human moral reality. They require this suspension in that they foster the expectation that surety in moral matters can be found — whether in feelings or in formulas — outside such a commitment to mutuality. This expectation, moreover, is one from which the moral educator is by no means immune, inasmuch as it is fostered by the fragmentation of the public realm, the effects of which none of our social contexts have managed to avoid. As a result, moral educators who do not acquiesce to either form of the demand to suspend critical moral dialogue can nonetheless be subject to temptations to "bad faith" on at least two levels. The first finds them employing the procedures of critical moral dialogue to support feelings or formulas. In submitting to this temptation, they are well on the way to becoming ideologues. The second finds them failing to place their own vision of mutuality to the test of critical dialogue. In submitting to this temptation, they are well on the way to considering themselves, or allowing others to consider them, gurus.

The moral educator who is subject to the demand to acquiesce to the end of critical dialogue, and to temptations to bad faith in conducting dialogue, is not just the classroom teacher; it is each of us. The most fundamental form in which moral education is conducted in any community, for youth and adult alike, is to be found in the practices of mutuality by which moral awareness is awakened and moral living is fostered in each of its social contexts. This fact makes it possible to subject contemporary concern for moral education to a test that can indicate whether it augurs well or ill for the reconstruction of a shared and shareable public realm. This test is a simple one: Is concern for moral education accompanied by an effective willingness to examine and, where needed, to reform the community's own practices, in its varied social contexts, for their adequacy in fashioning, fostering, and protecting human mutuality for each and for all?

If a community fails this test, its concern for moral education cannot function as an effective element of an effort to reconstruct a shared and shareable public realm. Such reconstruction can take place only in virtue of a commitment, fostered by the hope grounded in freedom, to the fulness of mutuality that is often only fitfully glimpsed in our practices. The role of moral education in such reconstruction is to discipline our imagination so that we develop the vision to catch sight of the human communalities that are signs of the mutuality to whose fulness we are destined. If a community proves unwilling to examine its own practices for their possibility of disclosing human communality and mutuality, its concern for moral education can become inimical to efforts to reconstruct a shared and shareable public realm. It can serve, instead, to entrench a community even further in its particularity over against a fragmented world.

This point has particularly telling ramifications for the direction of our efforts in moral education. It suggests that adults even more than the young are in need of reflective moral education. They are particularly in need of the disciplining of imagination to see the various contexts of human mutuality and communality in which they are placed. A lived acquiescence to the fragmentation of the public realm — which, for most of us, most of the time, accurately describes our modes of activity — generally blinds us to the possibility, let alone the need, of reflectively noting our placements in particular contexts of mutuality against larger backgrounds of human communality and human mutuality. We are married or we are single; we are parents; we are in business, we are church members, we are employed; we are military; we are professionals; we are in government. Occasionally we bump into situations that should bring to mind wider communalities and ties of mutuality: we are citizens, Christians, humans. In a fragmented public realm, the practices of our particular placements as married, or as business persons, or as professionals, generally make it increasingly difficult, first, to see clearly the demands that such larger communalities put upon our particular placements and, then, to interpet these demands as anything but onerous.

Moral Education: Imaginative Conversion

In these circumstances, the task of moral education for adults
is direct, necessary, but surely difficult. It is a task of imaginative
conversion: to make it possible to see our larger communalities
not as burdens but as invitations to extend the ken of our particular placements to a wider range of human mutuality. Once this
is seen, it may become possible to place those practices at the
service of these larger communalities and ties of mutuality. Placing these practices at the service of broader human communalities and ties of mutuality is not an easy task. It requires the
development and cultivation of a form of moral sensitivity that
is particularly fearsome because it functions to unmask us when
necessary: it is to pick out the various disguises in which self-
interest and special interest deck themselves out in these practices, in order to gain their way at the expense of others. These
disguises enable us to avoid looking at the denials of human communality involved in some of the practices of our particular placements. Practices for the preservation of public order can be blind
to the communality of our human vulnerability, of which we
ought to be reminded by each instance of needlessly inflicted
pain, even upon the wicked. Thus we countenance brutality in
the police and military, degradation in the practices of penal con-
finement, or even torture. Perhaps even worse, these disguises
permit us to acknowledge only the communalities that serve the
practices of our particular placements; thus we help the poor
only that they may become like us: consumers.

These disguises, and all like them, are nonetheless compati-
ble with a genuine concern that moral education shape the young
to rectitude of personal conduct. Herein lies a source of the unease I have with current interest in and discussion of moral education. That interest seems often to arise as a hope for practices
of moral education that will foster rectitude of personal moral
conduct among the young. Forms of moral education fashioned
in accord with this hope, however, need not ask us to place the
practices of our particular social contexts at the service of larger
human communalities and ties of mutuality; yet this is precisely
what we are asked to do by practices of moral education, whether
they are fashioned on the basis of a theory of moral development,
such as Kohlberg's, which makes justice the central moral con-

cept, or on the basis of a Christian theology, such as that of papal, conciliar, and episcopal documents, which makes the work of establishing and sustaining a just social order for all an essential element of each believing Christian's moral life. When justice is given moral centrality — whether it is in Kohlberg's terms as the focus of development of moral reasoning, or in theological terms, as the primary human social response to the proclamation of God's salvation — it requires us to foster practices of moral education of a kind different from those that seek only to ensure the rectitude of personal moral conduct.[14] The centrality of justice requires moral education to aim at sharpening perception of one's placement in particular social contexts and at developing skills for evaluating one's conduct and the practices of that conduct in terms of the larger and morally fundamental human mutuality we conceptualize as justice. The centrality of justice and the critical attention it requires us to pay to the public forms of our life with one another, therefore, can prove disappointing to expectations that the introduction of new practices in moral education should result in a better exhibition of rectitude in the personal conduct of the young. These practices will prove disappointing to such expectations because they are practices that make justice in our social contexts, not the rectitude of personal conduct, the main focus for judgments of the moral adequacy of human actions and practice.

Moral Education and our Vision of the Moral Future

Concern for moral education is a fundamental form in which a community exhibits its expectations for the moral future. The ambiguities in contemporary concern for moral education that this discussion has briefly brought to the surface indicate how fragile confidence in the moral future of an abiding community has become in a fragmented public realm. It has apparently become so fragile that it no longer seems clear to not a few Christians how the community can effectively hand on to the future the vision and the values that have shaped its life so far. This worry can have the ironic effect of distracting the community's attention from one activity that, although not sufficient to guarantee the effective handing on of vision, surely is necessary for it: the constant reappropriation of that vision to give critical guidance, not just to education, but to all forms of the community's practice and reflection. Such reappropriation can make it clear that a Christian vision of the moral future gives reason to question the adequacy of focusing concern about moral education simply upon the rectitude of personal moral conduct. That vision suggests that for practices of moral education to be adequate to the hope it offers for the abiding attainment of community, they be adopted out of a concern that is more encompassing of our human communality and, therefore, more fundamental to moral existence, than a concern that focuses only upon certain aspects of the conduct of the young. Practices of moral education can be adopted because they embody our hopes for a moral future that is, in part, constituted by the effort to fashion and sustain a just society. It should not be forgotten, moreover, that such practices, if they are faithful to the vision that informs them, will put the effectiveness of the community's hope for the moral future to the test. They will require that such hope be made concrete in practice by all individuals and institutions in their social contexts within the public realm. We should not be surprised if putting some of our practices to such a test proves disappointing with respect to hopes for a just society that the practices of moral education for justice can arouse: a fragmented public realm is marked by the disappearance of hopes for the future beyond the confines of particular social contexts, and by ambiguity and conflict in the hopes aroused by the practices of institutions and individuals in those contexts.

It is not necessary, of course, that such disappointment take place. It can be forestalled if practices of moral education function as part of a society's concrete commitment to work for justice in the present and for the moral future. Moral education would thereby serve as a challenge for youth to imagine the institutions and practices that, as adults, they will work together to fashion, in order to sustain in the public realm a vision of a just society. A soundly based concern for moral education, therefore, does not pose as its first question how the next generation is to learn how to be moral. It asks, rather, about the manner in which this generation has fashioned its moral existence. It asks about the adequacy of the practices and institutions of this generation for sustaining, for youth and adult alike, effective hope for a moral future of justice in a shared public realm.

V. PROFESSION, GIFT, AND SERVICE

Imagination: Power to Shape the World to Mutuality

I have argued throughout the course of this work for the importance of moral imagination. Moral imagination functions, under the tutelage of reason's interest in mutuality, to render us capable of envisioning a world in which the completion of human mutuality is possible. That world is not yet actual; its form is pledge and promise. Its form places upon us the demand that our actions and our practices bring this world to actuality.

The envisioning of a world in which the fulness of mutuality ought to be has a peculiar power with respect to human cravings. It enables our bearing toward these cravings to take on the character of receptivity to the bestowal of a "gift": we can envision these cravings as presented to us so that our actions and practices can bring about the completion of human mutuality that ought to be. Practices and actions that disclose the mutuality at the core of human freedom point out the possibility of envisioning our cravings as gifts. Friendship provides one paradigm of how our cravings, put to the service of mutuality, exhibit their character as gifts: friends "gift" one another by a mutual craving for shared understanding and trust. This craving serves as the threshold to a shared world.

My argument has insisted, however, that the practices of human mutuality are not by themselves capable of disclosing fully the character of our cravings as gifts. We are drawn to this disclosure as we become more and more aware that our human mutuality is thoroughly marked by finitude: our cravings, even envisioned as gifts, do not have power sufficient to bring our mutuality to its destined fulness. This lack of power grounds the importuning that our cravings make that their satisfaction be placed above the service of mutuality. Insofar as we take heed of the clamor of such importunity, we lessen the capacity our actions and practices have to bring about the fulness of human mutuality that ought to be. The envisioning of our cravings as gift is, as a result, a precarious enterprise. Finitude truncates our craving for mutuality so that the gifted character of all our cravings, which it has functioned to disclose, seems now a delusion: such gifted character would have us place all other cravings at the service of the one craving most surely doomed to frustration in consequence of our finitude: mutuality.

Precarious as it may be, an empowerment of imagination to see human craving as gift is something I have nonetheless maintained to take place. My argument has taken this empowerment to be, quite properly, a work of grace. Yet it is a work of grace to which we are rendered open by the hope whose ground is the exercise of our freedom. This empowerment takes place as the disclosure of the gifted character of human finitude itself: our finitude has evoked, from the side of the transcendent God, the gift of divine mutuality as the completion of human mutuality. By this empowerment, imagination is rendered capable of refashioning the world. It does so by determining how human practices may be shaped so that they serve mutuality and foster conditions for the attainment of its completion. The moral significance of human practice is thereby constituted through imagination: in virtue of the empowerment of imagination to envision our human cravings as gifts ordered to the service of mutuality, the freedom exercised in human practices is thus made effective for shaping the world to mutuality.

Transcendence: Freedom Made Effective for Mutuality

Human freedom can be exercised effectively for shaping the world to mutuality even when there has not yet been explicit acknowledgment that the response of God's transcendence to human finitude — that is, the invitation to share in God's mutuality — is the ground for the effectiveness of freedom.[15] Although explicit acknowledgment of its ground in God's transcendence is not required for the effectiveness of freedom, the particular practices in which freedom is exercised must nonetheless be capable of disclosing the role of imagination in making freedom effective for mutuality. In such disclosure, God's transcendence, inviting us to share in his mutuality as the ground of the empowering of freedom by imagination, can remain opaque to us. This is so because imagination effects a dual empowering of freedom for shaping a world of mutuality: an empowering of the freedom of faith, and an empowering of the freedom of moral endeavor. Empowering for the freedom of moral endeavor makes it possible for practices to give concrete shape to human mutuality. Once such mutuality begins to take shape, it then becomes possible for us to engage in these practices without fully adverting to the empowerment of imagination and, thereby, to the freedom of faith, which makes them capable of giving mutuality its concrete shape.

This absence of explicit notice of the role of imagination and its ground can be of relatively little consequence as long as we also engage in other practices that do keep us in mind explicitly of the function of imagination in empowering the freedom of faith for the freedom of moral endeavor. These are practices in which the empowerment by imagination of the freedom of faith makes it possible for us to see clearly that even in the face of our human finitude our human cravings can still be gift: they are anticipatory of the fulness of mutuality to which we are destined. This empowering of the freedom of faith then makes possible wholehearted engagement in practices for shaping the world to mutuality: such engagement marks our confidence that the fulness of mutuality will be accomplished, even though our finitude will render partial and incomplete each concrete form of mutuality effected through our moral endeavor.

This absence of explicit notice of the role of imagination and its ground is of far greater consequence when there is a breakdown of the practices that enable us to keep explicitly in mind its function for empowering the freedom of faith. These practices are the ones that nourish a community's awareness of the participation of each and all in a narrative of human life and human history ordered to the fulness of human mutuality — practices of its worship, artistic creation, scientific discovery, traditions of craft and of learning. As these practices cease to function as loci for public representations of a shared destiny toward the fulness of mutuality, other practices begin to lose contact with their own grounding in mutuality. This can be true even of those practices whose grounding in the service of mutuality has been most explicit. As a result, we find that in a fragmented public realm, which has as one of its chief manifestations the unavailability of public representations of a shared human destiny toward mutuality, the practices of various human professions — education, medicine, ministry, politics, and public service, to name a few — suffer loss of contact with their roots in the service of human mutuality.[16]

Symptomatic of this loss are the ways in which issues have been drawn in disputes about "professionalization" and about the rights and responsibilities of professions within the larger human community and its institutions. The concrete form these issues often take can be quite parochial; they are, frequently enough, pompous versions of jurisdictional disputes in the workplace. The issues most generally at stake, however, are of larger import: identity, power, skill, autonomy, and service.[17] The last-named is of fundamental importance in delimiting the proper relationship a profession bears to the other four: it is in virtue of placing one's skills at the service of each and all in the community that professional identity, autonomy, and power are accorded their due recognition. Even though this ordering to service is fundamental to "being professional," it seems to be employed less and less as a defining perspective for issues that bear upon professional life and activity.

Profession: Freedom Placed in the Service of Mutuality

Placing one's skills at the service of each and all in the community is a paradigmatic exercise of human mutuality. There is an acknowledgment of mutual trust in the worth of the skills and in the practitioner's ability, judgment, and integrity in employing them. However, in a community in which shared practices for publicly representing its hopes for a destiny in the fulness of mutuality are absent, the force of this paradigm is radically diminished. Professional identity, skill, power, and autonomy take on importance beyond that conferred in virtue of their ordering to the service of each and all in the community. As a result, they can be set over against the very mutuality that provides the paradigm for the initial recognition of their worth.

In such a community, professions can undergo reorientations of significant moral consequence. Their founding orientation of placing skills at the service of each and all can be transmuted into just one more interest to be weighed against the interests shaped by the other elements — identity, skill, autonomy, and power — in giving form to professional practices and policies. There is no assurance that policies shaped by this interplay of interests will be congruent with the founding orientation to service; as now only one aspect of a whole complex of professional interests, its normative force can no longer be overriding.

Indications of such reorientation have developed in various professions. To be sure, no profession has ever been free from practitioners willing to direct the employment of their skills primarily or exclusively toward the furtherance of their particular interests, even to the point of diminution or abandonment of service for each and for all in the community. There are, however, indications of a contemporary reorientation of a sort that has consequences potentially more wide-ranging than those that follow upon individual lapses from the orientation of one's profession to the service of each and all. These indications represent a loss of contact with the founding paradigm of mutuality in the very procedures by which a profession renders its skills to the service of the community. In many cases, the place of this founding paradigm has apparently been taken by a model of the marketplace: skills are to be placed in service insofar as they are, or can be made, "marketable."

Persuasive arguments could be made that the fundamental source of this reorientation is economic: professions such as education, medicine, and law have essentially become producers of services necessary for the proper functioning and expansion of a consumer economy.[18] Those arguments, however, would not pinpoint the moral anomaly of this reorientation. To do that, we must attribute this reorientation to failures, both within professions and within society at large, to nourish moral imagination by representations of human mutuality conducive to the formation of an ideal of service.

The renewed interest that many colleges and universities are now demonstrating in programs for continuing and adult education provides one instance of the moral anomaly involved in this reorientation. Few institutions would deny that their economic well-being or even survival is a prime factor for motivating such interest in reaching the "nontraditional" student. There is no doubt that many such programs can be of genuine service to the individuals who take part in them and to the communities in which they take place. When such programs are successful, one presumably could even claim that good has resulted simply from the coincidence of various paths along which particular interests were being pursued. Even so, it seems legitimate to raise the question: Why, in the past, did academia not see with such clarity and pursue with such vigor, this opportunity for placing its skills at the service of the community?

By raising this question I do not intend to overlook or to denigrate the longtime commitments many institutions, large and small, have had to adult and continuing education. I do hope to provoke some conscience-searching, however, that may note the irony of economic necessity leading to the "discovery" of non-traditional students. We surely cannot claim that they did not exist before; perhaps we just did not have the imagination to notice them and sense their desire for knowledge.

The irony I have noted here — that persons and institutions, shaped by an ideal that human desire for learning and knowledge is not fully satisfied even in a lifetime, should have taken recent note of the extent of that desire, not as a conclusion of that ideal, but out of the press of demographic and economic factors — is one I find significant, even though its particular manifestation here may not be the most urgent issue to confront our understanding of the function and moral significance of professions and their practice for the fashioning of a shared public realm. This irony touches directly upon one of the most fundamental features in the framing of any moral issue. In a relatively modest way it poses a question that crystalizes many of the concerns, of both moral theory and moral practice, that have informed this work. It raises the question: Who are the persons we see — who are the persons we are willing to take into account — when we desire, decide, and act?

Moral Imagination: Vision and Grace

Much of ill moral consequence takes place when we see no one at all, or only ourselves. Yet our imaginative capacity is strained when it is called beyond the ties of loyalty even of our widest particularisms — family, culture, nation, even church. I have been suggesting throughout this work that the call beyond particularisms is also a call through them: to see even in them the ofttimes faint marks of what is meant to be a shared human destiny of life with each other in the life of God. For the seeing we need help: God's grace, in the form of history, in our interdependence in community. For living in the face of what we see, we need help: images of our shared destiny made present to us in the assembly of worship. For the seeing and the living not to overwhelm us, we need help: prayer, and our quest for understanding. The last two are the ones that, by their very fragility, remind us most of our need for help, and give us most assurance of its presence.

From these, we take our bearings for the quest that is moral theology.

Notes

1. The Kingdom of God and the Kingdom of Ends

1. The phenomenon I term "philosophical eclecticism" can be understood as the analog, within Catholic moral theology, to the fragmentation of moral discourse which Alasdair MacIntyre points out as characteristic of modern philosophical ethics; see *After Virtue* (Notre Dame, Ind.: University of Notre Dame Press, 1981), pp. 1–34. I think it important to note, moreover, that philosophical eclecticism is instanced not only by picking and choosing those elements of various philosophical views which one then assembles to serve as a conceptual framework for moral theology; it is also instanced when one puts at the service of moral theology a single and coherent philosophical framework without elaborating the grounds for its claim to philosophical adequacy and soundness.

Instances of both forms of philosophical eclecticism can be found, I think, in one discussion which in recent years has occupied a prominent place in the literature of Catholic moral theology; this discussion has centered upon questions about the nature of moral norms and the ways in which such norms are grounded. Eclecticism is most apparent to me in the use to which the distinction between teleological and deontological theories has been put in efforts to deal with what seems to be the particular crux of the discussion: the possibility of exceptionless moral precepts or, more generally, moral "absolutes." This distinction has proved useful in clarifying certain options available to the moral theologian in trying to elaborate the conceptual framework for an account of moral norms; for example, it helps make clear that a deontological account of exceptionless moral precepts can be elaborated with greater conceptual economy than a teleological one can be; that clarification, of course, does not settle the question of whether or not there are such precepts. This distinction, however, does not help one determine whether a teleological framework is to be preferred to a deontological

177

one, or vice-versa, when one is trying not simply to render a coherent conceptual account of the scope of certain moral norms, but rather to offer an overall account of human moral life. Moreover, the distinction does not of itself provide clues to the means by which one's moral theory could coherently relate and even unify those elements of moral life that are conceptually contrasted by the distinction between teleology and deontology. That unity, in my judgment, can be provided only after one has elaborated an account of the basic character and structure of human agency and action. Thus the source of what I term "philosophical eclecticism" in moral theology may very well lie in a more fundamental disarray in philosophical efforts to provide a satisfactory account of human agency and personhood. Two recent works in which Catholic theologians have set forth the basic elements of their moral theories exhibit some of the consequences of this disarray. Timothy E. O'Connell recognizes the need for an account of human action and of the human person as one of the fundamental bases for moral theology; the account he gives, in Part II of *Principles for a Catholic Morality* (New York: Seabury, 1978), pp. 45–66, provides, at most, a sketchy justification of the major distinctions he makes in describing human capacities for knowing, choosing, and acting. Even though Daniel C. Maguire, in *The Moral Choice* (Garden City, N.Y.: Doubleday, 1978), makes "the experience of the value of persons and their environment" the foundation of morality (p. 72) and defines "moral" in terms of "what befits or does not befit persons as persons" (p. 71), he does not offer a systematic account of what it is about the reality of the person in virtue of which it has this founding value; in consequence, specifying what would concretely befit persons as persons becomes very difficult.

A number of the essays which have been important in the discussion of moral norms can be found in Charles E. Curran and Richard A. McCormick, eds., *Readings in Moral Theology No. 1: Moral Norms and the Catholic Tradition* (New York: Paulist, 1979). The essays in that volume by Bruno Schüller, "Various Types of Grounding for Ethical Norms," pp. 184–198; John R. Connery, "Morality of Consequences: A Critical Appraisal," pp. 244–266; Richard A. McCormick, "Reflections on the Literature," pp. 294–340; and Charles E. Curran, "Utilitarianism and Contemporary Moral Theology: Situating the Debates," pp. 341–362, explicitly place this discussion in the context of distinctions between teleological and deontological moral theories.

See also David Burrell, "Does Process Theology Rest on a Mistake?" *Theological Studies* 43 (1982): 125–135, for a thoughtful exposition of some of the factors at work in what I judge to be another manifestation of philosophical eclecticism in theology.

2. MacIntyre elaborates a point similar to this in his discussion of the narrative character of human identity; see *After Virtue*, pp. 190–209.

3. The works of Stanley Hauerwas and Enda McDonagh have suggested the appropriateness of terming human autonomy a "gift." See, for instance, Hauerwas, *A Community of Character: Toward a Constructive Christian Social Ethic* (Notre Dame, Ind.: University of Notre Dame Press, 1981), pp. 9–35, 129–152; McDonagh, *Gift and Call: Towards a Christian Theology of Morality* (Dublin: Gill & Macmillan, 1975), pp. 40–57, 76–89; and his *Doing the Truth: The Quest for Moral Theology* (Notre Dame, Ind.: University of Notre Dame Press, 1979), pp. 40–57, 76–89, 90–100.

4. MacIntyre, *After Virtue*, pp. 204–207, sketches a description of how our modern understanding of individuality has led us to see our concrete relations of mutuality only as limitations on our freedom. See also McDonagh, *Doing the Truth*, pp. 78–84.

5. A sophisticated contemporary version of this view is embodied in John Rawls's description in *A Theory of Justice* (Cambridge, Mass.: Harvard University, The Belknap Press, 1971), pp. 118–192, of an "original position" from which rational agents choose, as the basis for ordering their social institutions, that set of the principles of justice which Rawls elaborates. See Hauerwas, *A Community of Character*, pp. 77–83, for a particularly useful criticism of the moral presuppositions of the political tradition embodied in Rawls's account.

6. Much of the literature of contemporary Catholic moral theology has moved away from a dominant focus on what Enda McDonagh has described as "the pursuit of the nice distinction of sins within a basically legal framework which had a rational philosophical background and deferred to Scripture for token confirmation of its analysis" (*Doing the Truth*, p. 16) and thus seems less prone to take legality as the primary form in which to give the requirements of mutuality their public and institutional shape. Legality, however, is not the only form in which requirements of mutuality can be made to take a shape that puts them in opposition to the very freedom which is mutuality's foundation. One can formulate a moral theology in which the requirements of mutuality are placed in service to the particularisms of an ideology — even, with reduplicated irony, to an ideology of freedom — and thus limit the scope of freedom's exercise to just those activities which the ideology can legitimate. In resisting the lure of nostalgia for the security provided by making legality the primary shape for the requirements of mutuality, moral theology must take care not to box itself into the equally unsatisfactory particularisms that undergird ideologies.

7. Descartes's procedure of methodic doubt still retains a deep hold upon what we imagine to be the satisfactory resolution of intellectual inquiry; the standard of Cartesian indubitability is so high, however, that we are often willing to settle for "borrowing" certainty from occasions that seem to meet that standard. The philosophical discussion I

find most helpful for loosening the hold the Cartesian picture of certainty has on us is Ludwig Wittgenstein, *On Certainty*, trans. Denis Paul and G. E. M. Anscombe (New York: Harper & Row, 1972); see also Julian Hartt, *Theological Method and Imagination* (New York: Seabury, 1977), pp. 42–44.

8. See Hauerwas, *Vision and Virtue: Essays in Christian Ethical Reflection* (Notre Dame, Ind.: Fides, 1974, rpt. University of Notre Dame Press, 1981), pp. 93–110; *A Community of Character*, pp. 212–229; MacIntyre, *After Virtue*, pp. 30–34, 231–233; Iris Murdoch, *The Sovereignty of Good* (New York: Schocken, 1971), pp. 34–37, 79–80.

9. See Parker J. Palmer, *The Company of Strangers: Christians and the Renewal of America's Public Life* (New York: Crossroad, 1981), for a richly suggestive treatment of the notion of "public" which sees it as common ground for recognizing our likenesses and our differences and which proposes a central role for the church, particularly in terms of symbol and practice, in reconstituting a public realm.

10. *A Theory of Justice*, pp. 142–150.

11. Ibid., pp. 150–161, 161–183.

12. Both Hauerwas and MacIntyre have elaborated narrative's function in exhibiting the connection between freedom and mutuality; see for example, Hauerwas and David Burrell, "From System to Story: An Alternative Pattern for Rationality in Ethics" in Hauerwas, *Truthfulness and Tragedy: Further Investigations in Christian Ethics* (Notre Dame, Ind.: University of Notre Dame Press, 1977), pp. 15–39; Hauerwas, *A Community of Character*, pp. 9–35, 36–52, 196–211; MacIntyre, *After Virtue*, pp. 114–122, 190–209.

13. See, however, Alan Donagan, *The Theory of Morality* (Chicago: University of Chicago Press, 1977), for a particularly well-argued presentation for the adequacy of a moral theory that has as its fundamental principle respect for human beings as rational creatures.

14. *Republic* II 376E–III 392C, III 414B–415D.

15. See Hauerwas, *A Community of Character*, pp. 214–219; MacIntyre, *After Virtue*, pp. 60–75, 225–237.

16. See Hauerwas, *A Community of Character*, pp. 158–161, 165–166, 186–193; Palmer, *The Company of Strangers*, pp. 84–86.

17. Hauerwas, *Vision and Virtue*, pp. 222–240; *A Community of Character*, pp. 89–110. MacIntyre, *After Virtue*, 210–215; Philip Rossi, "Abortion and the Pursuit of Happiness," *Logos: Philosophic Issues in Christian Perspective* 3 (1982): 65–68.

18. For a discussion of the role of public worship for shaping a shared moral world see my article "Narrative, Worship, and Ethics: Empowering Images for the Shape of Christian Moral Life," *Journal of Religious Ethics* 7 (1979): 239–248; Hartt, *Theological Method and Imagination*, pp. 212–214. Palmer, *The Company of Strangers*, pp. 156–

163, indicates how private and liturgical prayer have an integral and complementary function in the church's efforts to refashion a public realm.

19. Aleksandr Solzhenitsyn, *The Nobel Lecture on Literature*, trans. Thomas P. Whitney (New York: Harper & Row, 1972); see Edward E. Ericson, Jr., *Solzhenitsyn: The Moral Vision* (Grand Rapids, Mich.: William B. Eerdmans, 1980), pp. 6–17; Hartt, *Theological Method and Imagination*, pp. 13–15; MacIntyre, *After Virtue*, pp. 210–211; Murdoch, *The Sovereignty of Good*, pp. 41, 84–88.

20. Some of the difficulties that an unqualified adoption of Kohlberg poses for Christian moral education are discussed by Paul Philibert, "Theological Guidance for Moral Development Research," in *Essays in Morality and Ethics*, ed. James Gaffney (New York: Paulist, 1980), pp. 106–125; see also Hauerwas, *A Community of Character*, p. 272; James A. O'Donohoe, "Moral and Faith Development Theory," in *Toward Moral and Religious Maturity*, ed. Christiane Brusselmans (Morristown, N.J.: Silver Burdett, 1980), pp. 385–392.

21. I have developed this interpretation in "Kant as a Christian Philosopher: Hope and the Symbols of Christian Faith," *Philosophy Today* 25 (1981): 24–33; "Kant's Doctrine of Hope: Reason's Interest and the Things of Faith," *The New Scholasticism* 56 (1982): 228–238 and "Moral Autonomy, Divine Transcendence and Human Destiny: Kant's Doctrine of Hope as a Philosophical Foundation for Christian Ethics," *The Thomist* 46 (1982): 441–458.

2. Imagination and the Truth of Morality

1. See Julian Hartt, *Theological Method and Imagination*, pp. 84–109, 219–254; Hauerwas, *Vision and Virtue*, pp. 68–89; *Truthfulness and Tragedy*, pp. 71–81; MacIntyre, *After Virtue*, pp. 30–32, 200–206.

2. I am not suggesting that there is only one philosophical approach in which such congruence, compatibility, and cooperation can be exhibited. In fact, the argument I present in this volume bears the mark of a variety of philosophical influences, particularly Kant, Aquinas, Wittgenstein, and Heidegger, who, with the obvious exception of Aquinas, might seem neither individually, nor collectively, readily congruent with Catholic theological tradition. I am suggesting, instead, that the confidence which the Catholic tradition has manifested in a cooperative relation between reason and faith should encourage a thoroughgoing development and exposition of a variety of philosophical approaches for their potential to serve as a sound and adequate conceptual basis for theological investigation. The encouragement of this kind of philosophical work could help end the phenomenon I have termed "philosophical eclecticism."

3. Hartt, *Theological Method and Imagination*, pp. 54–67, offers a useful diagnosis of the employment of social scientific categories in theology.

4. For the term "moral imagination" see Murdoch, *The Sovereignty of Good*, p. 37; I have tried to sketch out some of the elements of this notion in "Moral Imagination and the Narrative Modes of Moral Discourse," *Renascence* 31 (1979): 131–141 and "Moral Interest and Moral Imagination in Kant," *The Modern Schoolman* 57 (1980): 149–158.

5. *Critique of Practical Reason*, trans. Lewis White Beck (Indianapolis: Bobbs-Merrill, 1956), p. 30. Donagan, *The Theory of Morality*, pp. 207–208, offers a parallel case in a contemporary setting.

6. Niebuhr, *The Responsible Self: An Essay in Christian Moral Philosophy* (New York: Harper & Row, 1963), pp. 47–67.

7. Ibid., pp. 49–54.

8. Ibid., pp. 63–65, 79–84, 102–106, 121–126.

9. Hauerwas, *A Community of Character*, pp. 9–35; MacIntyre, *After Virtue*, pp. 205–207.

10. Doris Lessing, in *The Marriages Between Zones Three, Four and Five (As Narrated by the Chroniclers of Zone Three)* (New York: Random House, Vintage Books, 1981), recounts, in the form of a fable — within which storytelling and remembering play a central role — a tale in which man and woman struggle to find an appropriate way for likeness, difference, and particularity to have interplay in their relationship with one another.

11. Hauerwas has taken note of the significance the theme of welcoming the stranger has for the fundamental character of Christian ethics: *A Community of Character*, pp. 22–27, 92–93, 254; see also Palmer, *The Company of Strangers*, pp. 56–70. The foundational context that my argument takes such tales to delimit, however, suggests that the welcoming of the stranger is also of central import for moral theory in general; see Thomas W. Ogletree, "Hospitality to the Stranger," in *The American Society of Christian Ethics 1977 Selected Papers*, ed. Max L. Stackhouse (Waterloo, Ontario: The Council on the Study of Religion, 1977), pp. 16–40.

12. I have developed this point in "Moral Community, Imagination, and Human Rights: Philosophical Considerations on Uniting Traditions," in *Human Rights in the Americas: The Struggle for Consensus*, ed. Alfred Hennelly and John Langan (Washington, D.C.: Georgetown University Press, 1982), pp. 167–184.

13. A recent instance of this line of interpretation of Kant can be found in Carl Raschke, *Moral Action, God, and History in the Thought of Immanuel Kant* (Missoula, Mont.: Scholars Press, 1975). Gordon Kaufman, *The Theological Imagination: Constructing the Concept of God* (Philadelphia: Westminster, 1981), presents a well-articulated

account of the central philosophical basis for such an interpretation — namely, that human finitude is such that it requires that (our representation of) God be fashioned in accord with what is the (historically emergent) ideal of humanity. I take this view to be profoundly mistaken: it constitutes a radical denial of God's transcendence and entails the unintelligibility, if not the impossibility, of any form of revelation.

14. See H. R. Niebuhr, *The Responsible Self*, pp. 118–126; Michael Novak, *Ascent of the Mountain, Flight of the Dove: An Invitation to Religious Studies* (New York: Harper & Row, 1971), pp. 80–84; Ogletree, "Hospitality to the Stranger," pp. 26–27; Palmer, *The Company of Strangers*, pp. 43, 64–67.

15. One recent work of literature which exhibits this point is Doris Lessing's *The Marriages Between Zones Three, Four, and Five.* How stories are remembered, told, and heard is basic to the social fabric of the world she constructs in this fable. See also Hauerwas, *A Community of Character*, pp. 12–22.

16. See Donagan, *The Theory of Morality*, pp. 5–6, 9; the whole of Donagan's first chapter offers a number of enlightening observations about the relation between moral theory and the practice of traditional Hebrew-Christian morality. See also Kant, *Critique of Practical Reason*, pp. 30, 36–37, 94–95, and Louis Agosta, "Kant's Treasure Hard-to-Attain," *Kant-Studien* 69 (1978): 422–443, which provides a discussion of Kant's claim that untutored reason can grasp the "highest good." Of particular interest is the fact that Agosta sees narrative as a locus for the exhibition of untutored reason's grasp of this notion.

17. See, for instance, Solzhenitsyn's account of Anatoly Silin, in *The Gulag Archipelago 1918–1956: An Experiment in Literary Investigation V–VII*, trans. Harry Willetts (New York: Harper & Row, Perennial Library, 1979), pp. 105–109; his general reflections in *The Gulag Archipelago 1918–1956: An Experiment in Literary Investigation III–IV*, trans. Thomas P. Whitney (New York: Harper & Row, 1975), pp. 597–631.

18. See, for instance, *Gulag Archipelago III–IV*, pp. 65–66, 309–310, 623–624, 670–671.

19. A challenging interpretation of the way in which God's particularity is focused in most concrete terms in Jesus can be found in John Howard Yoder, *The Politics of Jesus* (Grand Rapids, Mich.: William B. Eerdmans, 1972), pp. 94–134.

20. See Hartt, *Theological Method and Imagination*, pp. 162–218, for a reflective and wide-ranging challenge to the ways in which questions about the historical character of Christian faith have been posed in much of contemporary theology.

21. Price, *A Palpable God: Thirty Stories Translated from the Bible*

with an Essay on the Origins and Life of Narrative (New York: Atheneum, 1978), pp. 13–14.

22. The classic contemporary treatment of the unifying role of charity in Catholic moral theology's account of the life of virtue is Gérard Gilleman, *The Primacy of Charity in Moral Theology*, trans. William F. Ryan and André Vachon (Westminster, Md.: Newman, 1959); see also McDonagh, *Invitation and Response: Essays in Christian Moral Theology* (New York: Sheed & Ward, 1972), pp. 59–78. The way in which love fosters mutuality has been developed in various ways; for instance, Charles E. Curran's "relationship-responsibility" model, *Catholic Moral Theology in Dialogue* (Notre Dame, Ind.: Fides, 1972, rpt. University of Notre Dame Press, 1976), pp. 150–183; *Moral Theology: A Continuing Journey* (Notre Dame, Ind.: University of Notre Dame Press, 1982), pp. 44–47, 69–74; Philip Keane's placing of the theory of "fundamental option" in the context of relations of love of God and of neighbor, *Sexual Morality: A Catholic Perspective* (New York: Paulist, 1977), pp. 35–40; Enda McDonagh's outline of the Christian ethic as a community ethic, *Invitation and Response*, pp. 38–58; and his sketch of the relation between Christian freedom and social ethics, *Doing the Truth*, pp. 90–100. While James Gustafson, *Protestant and Roman Catholic Ethics: Prospects for Rapproachment* (Chicago: University of Chicago Press, 1978), eschews developing an analysis of the use to which Roman Catholic moral theology has put the theme of love (p. 166), he does note ways in which contemporary analyses of the person stress mutuality and relation (pp. 87–92). For a different approach to the relation of person, virtue, and mutuality, see Hauerwas, *A Community of Character*, pp. 129–152.

23. See Joseph Fuchs, "The Absoluteness of Moral Terms," in Curran and McCormick, eds., *Readings in Moral Theology No. 1*, especially pp. 106–116; Gustafson, *Protestant and Roman Catholic Ethics*, pp. 90–94; O'Connell, *Principles for a Catholic Morality*, pp. 144–164. Central to this interpretation of nature is a consideration of its relation to, and insertion into, history.

24. I find this interpretation suggested by the work of R. S. Peters, whose writings offer a well-argued contemporary version of Hume's account of the moral sentiments; see, for instance, *Psychology and Ethical Development* (London: George Allen & Unwin, 1974), pp. 258–263, 291–302, 362–365, 400–405.

25. Rossi, "Moral Community, Imagination, and Human Rights: Philosophical Considerations on Uniting Traditions," in Hennelly and Langan, eds., *Human Rights in the Americas: The Struggle for Consensus*, pp. 175–183.

26. Palmer, *The Company of Strangers*, pp. 67–70.

27. H. Richard Niebuhr, *The Responsible Self*, pp. 79–89; *Radical*

Monotheism and Western Culture, with Supplementary Essays (New York: Harper & Brothers, 1960), offers an extended treatment of the way in which we can be rendered open, even in our particularities, toward that inclusiveness he terms "universal community." It is not clear, however, whether or not Niebuhr successfully avoids rendering human particularities into differences which are ultimately merely accidental.

28. *The Responsible Self*, pp. 47–68.

29. This may suggest why tragedy is one of the fundamental shapes which narrative takes. For tragedy to exhibit how our human communality is invited to transcend even the destructive and divisive possibilities that the human deeds recounted in the narrative make actual, there must be a fundmental engagement of human responsibility in such deeds. If this is so, then it seems that, even though Daniel Maguire has given recognition to the place of tragedy in the formation of the fundamental human moral perspective (*The Moral Choice*, pp. 341–369), he has not distinguished it sufficiently from suffering to show the core of its moral import. Hauerwas (*Truthfulness and Tragedy*, pp. 37–38, 67–70, 200–202), by placing tragedy in the context of human finitude and of the moral convictions which the narrative of our lives should display, is more accurate in locating for us tragedy's moral import.

3. Sure Hope

1. The interpretation of Kant developed in this and the next chapter is one which I initially proposed in the following articles: "Moral Interest and Moral Imagination in Kant," *The Modern Schoolman* 57 (1980): 149–158; "Kant as a Christian Philosopher: Hope and the Symbols of Christian Faith," *Philosophy Today* 25 (1981): 24–33; "Kant's Doctrine of Hope: Reason's Interest and the Things of Faith," *The New Scholasticism* 56 (1982): 228–238; "Moral Autonomy, Divine Transcendence and Human Destiny: Kant's Doctrine of Hope as a Philosophical Foundation for Christian Ethics," *The Thomist* 46(1982): 441–458.

2. See MacIntyre, *After Virtue*, pp. 22–75, for an account of the role Kant's philosophy played in the development of this understanding of the human agent and the agent's freedom. Iris Murdoch, *The Sovereignty of Good*, p. 80, has summed up well this picture: "Stripped of the exiguous metaphysical background which Kant was prepared to allow him, this man is with us still, free, independent, lonely, powerful, rational, responsible, brave, the hero of so many novels and books of moral philosophy." See also Hauerwas and Burrell, *Truthfulness and Tragedy*, pp. 16–27; Robert Paul Wolff, *The Autonomy of Reason* (New York: Harper & Row, 1973), pp. 181–187.

3. *Critique of Pure Reason*, trans. Norman Kemp Smith (New York: St. Martin's Press, 1929), A805/B833. Citations from the *Critique of*

Pure Reason are from the first (A) or second (B) German editions, as noted in the margins of Smith's translation.

4. Kant provides extensive discussion of the highest good in *Critique of Pure Reason*, A810–819/B838–847; *Critique of Practical Reason*, pp. 111–153. See also *Critique of Judgment*, trans. J. H. Bernard (New York: Hafner, 1951), pp. 284–286, 318–327; *Religion within the Limits of Reason Alone*, trans. Theodore M. Green and Hoyt H. Hudson; 2nd ed., revised and with an essay by John R. Silber (New York: Harper & Row, 1960), pp. 3–7.

5. *Critique of Practical Reason*, p. 133.

6. *Lectures on Philosophical Theology*, trans. Allen W. Wood and Gertrude M. Clark (Ithaca, N.Y.: Cornell University Press, 1978), p. 41.

7. For an elaboration of this point see my "Moral Interest and Moral Imagination in Kant" and "Kant's Doctrine of Hope: Reason's Interest and the Things of Faith."

8. *Religion within the Limits of Reason Alone*, p. 5.

9. See, for instance, *Critique of Practical Reason*, pp. 85, 89–90, 109–110; *Religion within the Limits of Reason Alone*, p. 86; *Critique of Judgment*, pp. 292–298.

10. See, for instance, James Collins, *The Emergence of Philosophy of Religion* (New Haven, Conn.: Yale University Press, 1967), pp. 150–152, 182–186; Michel Despland, *Kant on History and Religion* (Montreal: McGill-Queen's University Press, 1973), pp. 203–209; Allen W. Wood, *Kant's Moral Religion* (Ithaca, N.Y.: Cornell University Press, 1970), pp. 57–60, 74–78; Yirmiahu Yovel, *Kant and the Philosophy of History* (Princeton, N.J.: Princeton University Press, 1980), pp. 53–54, 64–66. Yovel, it should be noted, would not find this ordering of freedom to mutuality a basis for an affirmation of God.

11. The most familiar of these terms is "kingdom of ends" found in the *Groundwork of the Metaphysic of Morals*, trans. H. J. Paton (New York: Harper & Row, 1964), pp. 100–102. The expression "ethical commonwealth" appears in *Religion within the Limits of Reason Alone*, pp. 88–91; "kingdom of grace" in *Critique of Pure Reason*, A812/B840, A815/B843.

12. See Hauerwas, *A Community of Character*, pp. 77–86; *Vision and Virtue*, pp. 235–240; MacIntyre, *After Virtue*, pp. 146–150.

13. See Hauerwas, *A Community of Character*, pp. 83–86, 125–128, 223–229.

14. See, for instance, *Critique of Pure Reason*, A326–327/B382–383, A409–410/B436–437, A462–484/B490–512; *Critique of Practical Reason*, pp. 111–112; see also Martin Heidegger, *The Essence of Reasons*, trans. Terrence Malick (Evanston, Ill.: Northwestern University Press, 1969), pp. 41–91.

15. *Religion within the Limits of Reason Alone*, p. 4.

16. Ibid., p. 5.

17. *Critique of Practical Reason*, pp. 30–33, 42; *Critique of Judgment*, pp. 320–321.

18. *Critique of Practical Reason*, pp. 38, 123; see also *Religion within the Limits of Reason Alone*, p. 5; *Critique of Pure Reason*, A809–810/B837–838; Collins, *The Emergence of Philosophy of Religion*, pp. 151, 183–184; Despland, *Kant on History and Religion*, pp. 269–277.

19. The "social contract" tradition of moral philosophy seems to represent one effort to provide an image and narrative of the conditions under which the power of choice can be made to take such an interest. See Niebuhr, *The Responsible Self*, p. 73.

20. The following are some of the important texts for particular aspects of reason's interest:

a. The exhibition of reason's character as faculty of principles: *Critique of Pure Reason*, A299/B356, A462–476/B490–504, A547–557/B575–585, A797–819/B825–847; *Critique of Practical Reason*, pp. 74–92, 124; *Groundwork of the Metaphysic of Morals*, pp. 128–129.

b. The representations which exhibit reason's interest: *Critique of Pure Reason*, A419/B447 (freedom, world); A550–552/B578–580 (freedom); A580/B608 (God); A684–685/B712–713 (world); A685–686/B713–714 (God); *Critique of Practical Reason*, pp. 112–124 (highest good).

c. The use made of these representations: *Critique of Pure Reason*, A795–831/B823–859; *Critique of Practical Reason*, pp. 124–126, 137–153.

21. Hauerwas, *A Community of Character*, pp. 81–83, 214–219; MacIntyre, *After Virtue*, pp. 31–34, 68–69.

22. *Groundwork of the Metaphysic of Morals*, pp. 100–102.

23. See Ronald M. Green, *Religious Reason: The Rational and Moral Basis of Religious Belief* (New York: Oxford University Press, 1978), and Allen W. Wood, *Kant's Moral Religion*, for detailed discussions of Kant's exploration of the relation between moral faith and human finitude.

24. See *Critique of Pure Reason*, A813–814/B841–842; *Critique of Practical Reason*, pp. 114–117; *Religion within the Limits of Reason Alone*, pp. 3–7.

25. *Critique of Practical Reason*, pp. 63–64, 114–115; *Religion within the Limits of Reason Alone*, pp. 5n–7, 31–32, 41n–42.

26. *Critique of Practical Reason*, pp. 117, 129, 133–134; *Critique of Pure Reason*, A808–810/B837–838; see Green, *Religious Reason*, pp. 55–60; Wood, *Kant's Moral Religion*, pp. 52–60.

27. *Critique of Practical Reason*, pp. 114–115, 131–134; see Collins, *The Emergence of Philosophy of Religion*, pp. 150–151, 173–175.

28. "Givenness" in the mode of sensibility is suggested as a mark of the finitude of reason in its theoretical use by the remarks Kant makes about the character of intellectual intuition as original, *Critique of Pure Reason*, B71–72; see Jürgen Habermas, *Knowledge and Human Inter-*

ests, trans. Jeremy J. Shapiro (Boston: Beacon Press, 1971), pp. 198–205; Martin Heidegger, *Kant and the Problem of Metaphysics,* trans. James S. Churchill (Bloomington: Indiana University Press, 1962), pp. 31–39. "Givenness" as a mark of the finitude of reason in its practical use is exhibited by freedom as a "fact" of reason: *Critique of Practical Reason,* pp. 31, 43; *Critique of Judgment,* pp. 320–321. "Givenness" of the structure of desire as it is ordered to the attainment of happiness provides one of the grounds generating the antinomy of practical reason: *Critique of Practical Reason,* pp. 114–115, 117–124; the resolution of the antinomy rests upon the proper ordering of the interests of finite human reason in its theoretical and practical uses: *Critique of Practical Reason,* pp. 124–126, 139–142.

29. *Critique of Judgment,* pp. 321–323.

4. Image and Gift

1. See MacIntyre, *After Virtue,* pp. 65–66, for one statement of the predicament into which contemporary moral discourse and public practice have fallen in consequence of this way of conceiving the core of the moral agent's freedom.

2. See Collins, *The Emergence of Philosophy of Religion,* p. 184: "Kant's correlation between the question about hope and the religious response can now be considerably sharpened. The generating question itself for religion concerns not only what *I* may hope by myself, but more determinatively and incisively, what *we* may hope together, as fellow men and bearers of the tendency toward personality. And the proportionate religious response bears upon God precisely as the Lord of the ethical commonwealth, as the common hope for men who are striving together to realize a social good which may not entirely lie within human power." See also Despland, *Kant on History and Religion,* pp. 223–226.

3. See Hartt, *Theological Method and Imagination,* pp. vii–xvi, 1–11, 60–67, 147–151, 189–218.

4. *Critique of Practical Reason,* pp. 89–92; compare Collins, *The Emergence of Philosophy of Religion,* pp. 184–189, 191–204, with Raschke, *Moral Action, God, and History in the Thought of Immanuel Kant,* pp. 150–162, for divergent interpretations of the way in which the human person is "elevated" by membership in a kingdom of ends.

5. See MacIntyre, *After Virtue,* pp. 175–189, 210–222; Hauerwas, *A Community of Character,* pp. 125–128; Palmer, *The Company of Strangers,* pp. 20–22, 46–55.

6. See Hauerwas, *A Community of Character,* pp. 136–141, 143–145, 148–152. Iris Murdoch's discussion in *The Sovereignty of Good,* pp. 16–45, suggests the possibility that one can engage in these prac-

tices without seeing — or seeing clearly — the reality in which they are constituted.

7. See Gustafson, *Can Ethics Be Christian?* (Chicago: University of Chicago Press, 1975), pp. 48–81; McDonagh, *Doing the Truth*, pp. 23–24, 48–56, and *Gift and Call: Towards a Christian Theology of Morality*, pp. 29–37, 43–62; H. Richard Niebuhr, *The Responsible Self*, pp. 115–126.

8. Two examples of contemporary moral theory's placing of all human cravings on an equal footing can be found in R. M. Hare, *Freedom and Reason* (Oxford: Oxford University Press, 1963), pp. 118–125; Rawls, *A Theory of Justice*, pp. 90–95, 126–130, 407–424. It is significant that each of these accounts generally tries to make purely formal the grounds on which any moral assessment of desires can be legitimately offered. For a criticism of such an account of desires see Hauerwas, *A Community of Character*, pp. 77–83, 215–219.

9. One ground on which talk of "rational craving" can be based is Kant's identification of will with practical reason; see *Critique of Practical Reason*, pp. 15–16, 32–33. *The Metaphysical Elements of Justice: Part I of the Metaphysics of Morals*, trans. John Ladd (Indianapolis: Bobbs-Merrill, 1964), pp. 10–14, presents Kant's account of the relation between will and desire. This identification makes it possible to see Kant's accounts of religion and morality as standing within an Augustinian tradition; see William Barrett, *The Illusion of Technique* (Garden City, N.Y.: Doubleday, 1978), p. 247: "The Kantian good will, which wills to submit itself to the moral law, is a descendant of the *voluntas*, the will in St. Augustine, which is restless until it rests in God." See also Karl Barth, *Protestant Theology in the Nineteenth Century: Its Background and History* (Valley Forge, Pa.: Judson, 1973), pp. 272–278.

10. Karl Rahner, *Foundations of Christian Faith: An Introduction to the Idea of Christianity*, trans. William V. Dych (New York: Seabury, 1978), seems to suggest this in his remarks on freedom, dependence, and salvation in history (pp. 35–43). See also Collins, *The Emergence of Philosophy of Religion*, pp. 198–204, who sees Kant's discussion of human freedom's role in history ordering it to a fidelity whose hope is focused upon the fulfillment of human community.

11. See Rahner, *Foundations of Christian Faith*, pp. 78–79, 140–142.

12. To the extent that this hope is unpersuasive, contractarian accounts of human moral life become plausible. See Hauerwas, *A Community of Character*, pp. 81–83, 159–161; MacIntyre, *After Virtue*, pp. 232–233; Niebuhr, *The Responsible Self*, pp. 98–100, 106–107, 141–142.

13. Brian O. McDermott, "Power and Parable in Jesus' Ministry," in *Above Every Name: The Lordship of Christ and Social Systems*, ed. Thomas E. Clarke (Ramsey, N.J.: Paulist, 1980), pp. 83–104, interprets

the power of Jesus' parabling to be that of an imaginative "world-reversal" which exhibits Jesus' own surrender in trust to his Father; in consequence the Christian is called to be also a parabler — i.e., to exhibit the same imaginative empowerment, grounded in trust, in his or her life.

14. A development of this point might provide a basis on which the Trinitarian character of Christian moral life could be elaborated. McDonagh, *Doing the Truth*, pp. 37–38, 45–47, 58–60; and Gilbert Meilander, *Friendship: A Study in Theological Ethics* (Notre Dame, Ind.: University of Notre Dame Press, 1981), pp. 51–52, take note of the possibility of interpreting the shape of Christian moral existence in Trinitarian terms.

15. Collins, *The Emergence of Philosophy of Religion*, pp. 151–152: "Belief in God is an assent to him precisely as a transcendent and morally concerned person, whose creative power not only originates the orders of nature and morality, but also assures the ultimate achievement of moral ends in the natural and social worlds." See also ibid., pp. 182–184; Despland, *Kant on History and Religion*, pp. 224–226, 263–269.

16. I am using the term "practice" as a generic designation for the activities and patterns of conduct by which we acquire what Hauerwas calls the "skills" for understanding and negotiating our moral and religious existence truthfully; see *Truthfulness and Tragedy*, pp. 8–12, 76–81; *A Community of Character*, pp. 9–12, 49–51, 125–128.

17. See Rossi, "Kant's Doctrine of Hope: Reason's Interest and the Things of Faith," for a discussion of how hope functions, within Kant's account of human moral existence, as practical reason in the mode of expectation; see also Collins, *The Emergence of Philosophy of Religion*, pp. 199–204.

18. The attentiveness which this imaginative power enables may be particularly crucial for a community's ability to see what it once may have considered a "prophetic" stance — for example, non-violence — as now gifting the community with an invitation to fashion new practices, or to refashion its old practices, in a way which more fully exhibits the pledge that fulness of mutuality is our human destiny; see McDonagh, *Doing the Truth*, pp. 138–152; *Gift and Call*, pp. 159–166.

19. See Hartt, *Theological Method and Imagination*, pp. 193–195, 236–248; Hauerwas, *Vision and Virtue*, pp. 30–47; Murdoch, *The Sovereignty of Good*, pp. 41–45, 64–70.

20. See Palmer, *The Company of Strangers*, p. 20.

21. Hegel has provided, in my judgment, the central philosophical articulation of this hope for overcoming finitude; see Collins, *The Emergence of Philosophy of Religion*, pp. 254–266, 293–299, 401–406. G. Kaufman, in *The Theological Imagination: Constructing the Concept of God*, offers what I take to be a contemporary rendering of the He-

gelian hope for an immanent human transcending of human finitude. Allen W. Wood, *Kant's Rational Theology* (Ithaca, N.Y.: Cornell University Press, 1978), pp. 147–151, makes some quite helpful remarks about Kant's own views on the relation between human finitude and the traditional scholastic-rationalist conception of God and about the conceptual strength of Kant's views in relation to certain post-Kantian analyses that have often found favor in contemporary theology.

22. Reynolds Price, *A Palpable God*, p. 25, suggests this by noting its converse: "Only the story which declares our total incurable abandonment is repugnant and will not be heard for long."

5. Hope, Community, and Worship

1. Hauerwas and Burrell, *Truthfulness and Tragedy*, pp. 16–27; MacIntyre, *After Virtue*, pp. 30–32, 205; Murdoch, *The Sovereignty of Good*, pp. 6–9.

2. The public character of fidelity and its connection with the significance of time for human moral endeavor was suggested by Hauerwas, *A Community of Character*, pp. 165–166, 186–193. For more general considerations on the rooting of human fidelity in God's fidelity see John C. Haughey, *Should Anyone Say Forever? On Making, Keeping and Breaking Commitments* (Garden City, N.Y.: Doubleday, 1975), pp. 150–166.

3. See Hauerwas, *A Community of Character*, pp. 81–82, 162–165, 168–171.

4. Haughey, *Should Anyone Say Forever?* pp. 7–14, 61–86.

5. For some general considerations on the image of covenant and its significance for shaping Christian moral life see, for instance, Bernard Häring, *Free and Faithful in Christ: Moral Theology for Clergy and Laity*, Vol. I: *General Moral Theology* (New York: Seabury, 1978), pp. 7–22; McDonagh, *Invitation and Response: Essays in Christian Moral Theology*, pp. 41–47, 97–98; O'Connell, *Principles for a Catholic Morality*, p. 21; Paul Ramsey, *Basic Christian Ethics* (New York: Charles Scribner's Sons, 1953), pp. 2–24, 367–388. For particular connections between God's covenant fidelity and human fidelity, see Haughey, *Should Anyone Say Forever?* pp. 157–166; Keane, *Sexual Morality: A Catholic Perspective*, pp. 10, 93–95; McDonagh, *Doing the Truth*, pp. 172–173; Ramsey, "Liturgy and Ethics," *The Journal of Religious Ethics* 7 (1979): 152–160.

6. See Baruch Brody, *Abortion and the Sanctity of Human Life: A Philosophical View* (Cambridge, Mass.: MIT Press, 1975), pp. 26–39, and Edward R. Langerak, "Abortion: Listening to the Middle," *The Hastings Center Report* 9, no. 5 (October 1979): 24–28, for two useful summaries of arguments about abortion which use the language of

"rights and claims." For discussions which challenge setting the arguments principally in these terms see Larry R. Churchill and José Jorgé Simán, "Abortion and the Rhetoric of Individual Rights," *Hastings Center Report* 12, no. 1 (February 1982): 9–12; Hauerwas, *A Community of Character*, pp. 212–229, and *Vision and Virtue*, pp. 147–165; and my "Abortion and the Pursuit of Happiness," *Logos: Philosophic Issues in Christian Perspective* 3 (1982): 61–77, and "'Rights' Are Not Enough: Prospects for a New Approach to the Morality of Abortion," *Linacre Quarterly* 46 (1979): 109–117.

7. See Hauerwas, *A Community of Character*, pp. 201–211.

8. See MacIntyre, *After Virtue*, pp. 210–237. Palmer, *The Company of Strangers*, pp. 52–54, notes the formative role the image "covenant" has historically played — and now seemingly lost — in American understanding of the public realm in which common good is fashioned.

9. See Donald J. Keefe, "Toward a Eucharistic Morality," *Communio* 2 (1975): 104–107, 114–116; McDonagh, *Doing the Truth*, pp. 45–47, and *Invitation and Response*, pp. 96–97, 106•108; D. E. Saliers, "Liturgy and Ethics: Some New Beginnings," *Journal of Religious Ethics* 7 (1979): 183–186.

10. Ramsey, "Liturgy and Ethics," uses a geometric image — the *convex* of God's action determining the *concave* shape of Christian liturgies — to speak of the way in which the disclosure of who God is engenders recognition of who we are.

11. See Kenneth Smits, "A Congregational Order of Worship," *Worship* 54 (1980): 55–75 for a discussion of how new liturgical forms have placed this kind of responsibility upon each and all who are gathered to worship.

12. Although MacIntyre does not propose acquiescence to this fragmentation of the public realm, he has yet to spell out the character of the public realm in which he hopes that we will be capable of sharing; see *After Virtue*, pp. 238–245. Hauerwas, moreover, appears even less ready to offer a proposal by which the narratives that give shape to the moral existence of Christians can serve to open the possibility of fashioning a public realm in and for the "world" in which Christians and their church dwell; see *A Community of Character*, pp. 83–86, 101–110. His reluctance to allow the church to embark on such an enterprise is understandable in the light of Reformation traditions that picture the relations between faith and reason, grace and nature, in ways different from those characteristic of Catholic traditions. In view of what was said in Chapter 2 about the confidence that Catholic theology has generally had in the possibilities for the congruence, compatibility, and cooperation of faith and reason — particularly if we recover and renew for reason the rich and varied life which much of twentieth-century philosophy has denied it — I do not share Hauerwas's reserve

about the appropriateness of a Christian community's engagement in efforts to fashion a public realm.

13. See MacIntyre's discussion of emotivism, *After Virtue*, pp. 6–34, for a helpful account of how privatized choice has come to function as the unassailable moral criterion for our age.

14. Even though Kohlberg's focus on justice would seem to imply an ordering of moral concerns toward human social reality, his theory has been criticized for not having sufficiently recast the highly individualistic image of moral agency characteristic of classical liberal political theory, and thus for neglecting important aspects of human social existence; see, for instance, Carol Gilligan, "Justice and Responsibility: Thinking About Real Dilemmas of Moral Conflict and Choice," in *Towards Moral and Religious Maturity*, ed. Brusselmans, pp. 223–249, and McDonagh, "Moral Theology and Moral Development," ibid., pp. 319–342. In the latter article, pp. 329–333, McDonagh notes some problems involved in shifting the focus of moral education to the community context of human moral existence.

15. This distinction that can be made between God's mutuality as ground for freedom's effectiveness and the possibilities both for exhibiting and acknowledging it may be of relevance to discussion of the question of the extent to which a distinctive character can be attributed to Christian ethics and conduct; see Gustafson, *Can Ethics Be Christian?*, pp. 169–179.

16. See Michael Bayles, *Professional Ethics* (Belmont, Calif.: Wadsworth, 1981), pp. 7–9, and Hauerwas, *Truthfulness and Tragedy*, pp. 189–190, for summaries of the most widely accepted set of characteristics which constitute a "profession." There are three particular characteristics of a profession that make it vulnerable to those forces of fragmentation depicted by MacIntyre (*After Virtue*, pp. 60–83) that make the central "characters" of modern society the aesthete, the therapist, and the manager. These characteristics are the possession of skills (or "expertise"), the ordering of those skills to the attainment of good(s) necessary for human life in society, and the self-governance (or autonomy) of the profession. To the extent that professions have sustained a tradition that allows the placing of their particular skills and the good they enable in the context of a larger vision of public good, they have been able to withstand the full impact of the forces MacIntyre describes. As Hauerwas points out, however, there is little reason to think that in a moral world as fragmented as ours these professions will be able, by themselves, to sustain for us all — or even for their own members — the moral coherence provided by a larger vision of public good; see *A Community of Character*, p. 126. See Palmer, *The Company of Strangers*, pp. 97–99, for a sketch of what can happen to a profession when there is lack of an adequate public realm.

17. See George Agich, "Professionalism and Ethics in Health Care," *Journal of Medicine and Philosophy* 5 (1980): 186–199.

18. Concomitant to the reorientation of "traditional" professions to a market model, there has been a proliferation of "new" professions, so that in 1970, 14.5 percent of the workforce in the United States could be classified as professional or technical workers; see Bayles, *Professional Ethics*, p. 4.

Index